CW00481238

Super Easy Air Fryer Cookbook for Beginners 2023

1900 Days of Easy, Budget-Friendly, and Mouthwatering Air Fryer Recipes to Transform Your Cooking Experience, Perfect for Weeknight Meals

Jude Barton

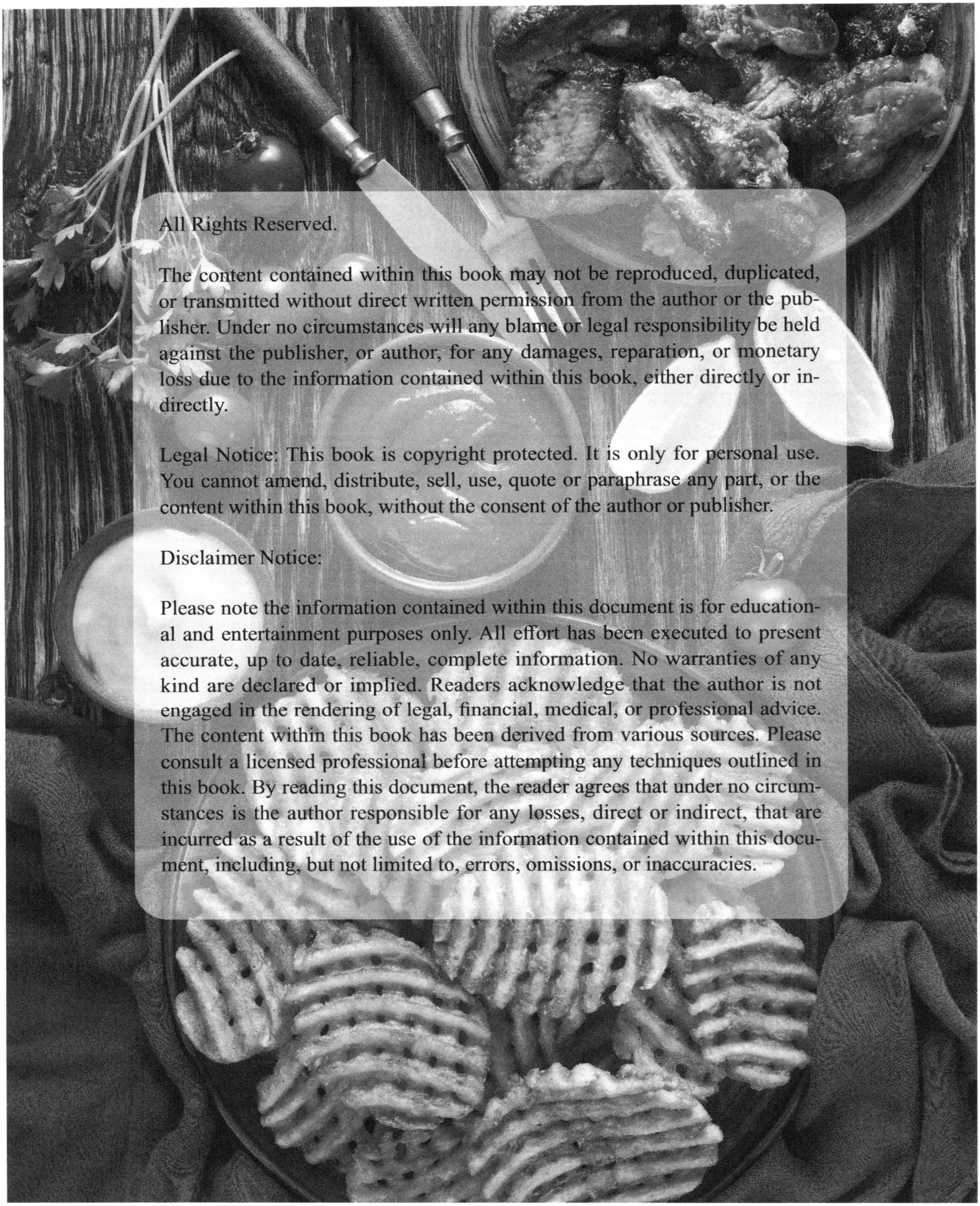

CONTENTS

INTRODUCTION

Jude Barton, a culinary maestro in his own right, needs little introduction for those familiar with the contemporary food scene. His prowess in the kitchen, combined with his penchant for healthful, yet delectable cooking, makes him the perfect guide for this journey into the universe of Air Fryer. Jude's connection with food is not just about techniques and recipes—it's a dance of passion, creativity, and the sheer joy of savoring life's delightful flavors.

At the core of this cookbook is a philosophy that many might have thought contradictory before: that indulgence and health are not opposing forces. The Air Fryer stands as a testament to this belief. By using superheated air to cook food, it mimics the crispy, tantalizing results of deep frying, without the excess oils and fats. And in Jude's adept hands, this tool becomes an orchestra, producing symphonies of flavors that are both nutritious and delicious.

But this book is more than just a collection of recipes. It is a testament to Jude Barton's belief in the democratic nature of good food—that gourmet doesn't have to mean inaccessible or complicated. Each recipe is crafted with the home cook in mind: easy to follow, quick to prepare, and using ingredients that are readily available. From the busy parent looking for a quick weeknight dinner solution to the enthusiastic foodie eager to try their hand at a new cooking technique, there's something in this cookbook for everyone.

In the following pages, you'll discover a plethora of dishes—ranging from the comfort of classic favorites to the excitement of avant-garde creations. With Jude's guidance, the humble Air Fryer is elevated from a mere appliance to an instrument of culinary magic.

How can this Air Fryer cookbook change your diet?

Healthier Cooking Methods

The primary appeal of an Air Fryer is that it allows for frying foods with minimal to no oil, which translates to fewer calories and less unhealthy fats in meals. By following the recipes in the cookbook, individuals can enjoy their favorite fried dishes with a fraction of the guilt and health risks.

Variety of Choices

The Air Fryer cookbook isn't just about fried foods. It includes recipes ranging from baked goods to grilled dishes, expanding one's culinary horizons and encouraging a well-rounded diet.

Portion Control

The design of most Air Fryers promotes cooking in smaller batches, which can help individuals become more mindful of portion sizes, reducing the chances of overeating.

Reduction in Processed Food

With a plethora of recipes at one's fingertips, individuals might feel more inclined to cook fresh meals at home rather than relying on store-bought, processed alternatives. This shift can lead to a reduction in sodium, preservatives, and unhealthy additives in one's diet.

Incorporation of Whole Food

Many Air Fryer cookbook recipes emphasize the use of whole, unprocessed ingredients, which are inherently healthier and more nutrient-dense. This can lead to a more balanced and nutritionally sound diet.

Time and Energy Efficiency

The quick cooking times associated with air frying can make it easier for individuals to prepare home-cooked meals even on busy days. This convenience can discourage unhealthy fast-food options, fostering a consistent healthy eating habit.

What Air Fryer food collection is offered in this cookbook?

1. **Appetizers and Snacks**: From crispy Brussels sprouts to zucchini fries, these light bites are perfect for kickstarting any meal or enjoying on their own. Think of golden-brown mozzarella sticks or flavorful stuffed mushrooms.

2. **Main Courses**: Whether it's succulent chicken thighs with a crispy skin, a juicy burger, or flaky salmon fillets, the Air Fryer can do it all. There might be dishes like lemon herb chicken, BBQ pork chops, or even herb-crusted lamb racks.

3. **Vegetarian and Vegan Delights**: Dishes that highlight the earthy richness of vegetables, such as crispy tofu bites, stuffed bell peppers, or cauliflower buffalo wings.

4. **Side Dishes**: These would complement any main course, ranging from garlic roasted asparagus to air-fried sweet potato wedges or parmesan-crusted green beans.

5. **Breads and Pastries**: From homemade bagels to soft and fluffy doughnuts, these baked goods are surprisingly easy to whip up in an Air Fryer.

6. **Breakfast Choices**: Start your morning right with quick-fix recipes like French toast sticks, breakfast burritos, or even omelette bites.

7. **Dips and Sauces**: These accompany the main and side dishes, offering recipes for tangy, spicy, sweet, or creamy accompaniments to enhance the flavor of air-fried foods.

How to get the most out of your Air Fryer?

- **Understand its Strengths**

Recognize that while the Air Fryer is fantastic for frying with less oil, it's also great for roasting, baking, and even grilling some foods.

- **Preheat the Fryer**

Although not always necessary, preheating your Air Fryer for a few minutes can help achieve a consistent cooking temperature and better results.

- **Avoid Overcrowding**

Place food in a single layer to ensure even cooking. If you're cooking larger batches, consider cooking in stages or shaking the basket periodically for even heat distribution.

- **Use the Right Oil**

While the Air Fryer requires less oil, using a small amount of the right oil can enhance the crispiness. Spray oils are perfect for a light, even coat. Choose oils with higher smoke points, like avocado or grapeseed oil.

- **Clean Regularly**

Regular cleaning avoids flavor contamination and ensures longevity. Remove leftover food particles, and clean the drawer, basket, and inside after every use.

- **Be Mindful of Cooking Time**

Since the Air Fryer cooks faster than traditional ovens, regularly check the food to prevent overcooking.

- **Use Marinades and Seasonings**

Flavor your food before air frying with rubs, marinades, or seasonings to enhance taste.

- **Avoid Aerosol Sprays**

Some aerosol sprays can damage the non-stick coating of the Air Fryer basket. Instead, use oil in a pump sprayer or brush it on.

- **Layer with Parchment**

For foods that might stick, consider using perforated parchment paper made for Air Fryers. This ensures easy food removal and aids in cleanup.

- **Stay Safe**

Avoid touching the interior while in use, and give it time to cool before cleaning. If you're cooking fatty foods, regularly check the drip tray and empty excess fat to prevent smoke.

- **Use it Regularly**

Don't reserve your Air Fryer for "frying" alone. Try roasting veggies, baking muffins, or reheating leftovers to get the most out of your appliance.

APPENDIX : Measurement Conversions

BASIC KITCHEN CONVERSIONS & EQUIVALENTS

DRY MEASUREMENTS CONVERSION CHART

3 TEASPOONS = 1 TABLESPOON = 1/16 CUP

6 TEASPOONS = 2 TABLESPOONS = 1/8 CUP

12 TEASPOONS = 4 TABLESPOONS = 1/4 CUP

24 TEASPOONS = 8 TABLESPOONS = 1/2 CUP

36 TEASPOONS = 12 TABLESPOONS = 3/4 CUP

48 TEASPOONS = 16 TABLESPOONS = 1 CUP

METRIC TO US COOKING CONVERSIONS

OVEN TEMPERATURES

120 °C = 250 °F

160 °C = 320 °F

180° C = 350 °F

205 °C = 400 °F

220 °C = 425 °F

LIQUID MEASUREMENTS CONVERSION CHART

8 FLUID OUNCES = 1 CUP = 1/2 PINT = 1/4 QUART

16 FLUID OUNCES = 2 CUPS = 1 PINT = 1/2 QUART

32 FLUID OUNCES = 4 CUPS = 2 PINTS = 1 QUART

= 1/4 GALLON

128 FLUID OUNCES = 16 CUPS = 8 PINTS = 4 QUARTS = 1 GALLON

BAKING IN GRAMS

1 CUP FLOUR = 140 GRAMS

1 CUP SUGAR = 150 GRAMS

1 CUP POWDERED SUGAR = 160 GRAMS

1 CUP HEAVY CREAM = 235 GRAMS

VOLUME

1 MILLILITER = 1/5 TEASPOON

5 ML = 1 TEASPOON

15 ML = 1 TABLESPOON

240 ML = 1 CUP OR 8 FLUID OUNCES

1 LITER = 34 FL. OUNCES

WEIGHT

1 GRAM = .035 OUNCES

100 GRAMS = 3.5 OUNCES

500 GRAMS = 1.1 POUNDS

1 KILOGRAM = 35 OUNCES

US TO METRIC COOKING CONVERSIONS

1/5 TSP = 1 ML

1 TSP = 5 ML

1 TBSP = 15 ML

1 FL OUNCE = 30 ML

1 CUP = 237 ML

1 PINT (2 CUPS) = 473 ML

1 QUART (4 CUPS) = .95 LITER

1 GALLON (16 CUPS) = 3.8 LITERS

1 OZ = 28 GRAMS

1 POUND = 454 GRAMS

BUTTER

1 CUP BUTTER = 2 STICKS = 8 OUNCES = 230 GRAMS = 8 TABLESPOONS

WHAT DOES 1 CUP EQUAL

1 CUP = 8 FLUID OUNCES

1 CUP = 16 TABLESPOONS

1 CUP = 48 TEASPOONS

1 CUP = 1/2 PINT

1 CUP = 1/4 QUART

1 CUP = 1/16 GALLON

1 CUP = 240 ML

BAKING PAN CONVERSIONS

1 CUP ALL-PURPOSE FLOUR = 4.5 OZ

1 CUP ROLLED OATS = 3 OZ 1 LARGE EGG = 1.7 OZ

1 CUP BUTTER = 8 OZ 1 CUP MILK = 8 OZ

1 CUP HEAVY CREAM = 8.4 OZ

1 CUP GRANULATED SUGAR = 7.1 OZ

1 CUP PACKED BROWN SUGAR = 7.75 OZ

1 CUP VEGETABLE OIL = 7.7 OZ

1 CUP UNSIFTED POWDERED SUGAR = 4.4 OZ

BAKING PAN CONVERSIONS

9-INCH ROUND CAKE PAN = 12 CUPS

10-INCH TUBE PAN =16 CUPS

11-INCH BUNDT PAN = 12 CUPS

9-INCH SPRINGFORM PAN = 10 CUPS

9 X 5 INCH LOAF PAN = 8 CUPS

9-INCH SQUARE PAN = 8 CUPS

Breakfast & Snacks And Fries Recipes

Polenta Fries

Servings: 6
Cooking Time:xx
Ingredients:

- 800 ml/scant 3½ cups water
- 1½ vegetable stock cubes
- ¾ teaspoon dried oregano
- ¾ teaspoon freshly ground black pepper
- 200 g/1⅓ cups quick-cook polenta/cornmeal
- 2 teaspoons olive oil
- 55 g/6 tablespoons plain/all-purpose flour (gluten-free if you wish)
- garlic mayonnaise, to serve

Directions:

1. Bring the water and stock cubes to the boil in a saucepan with the oregano and black pepper. Stir in the polenta/cornmeal and continue to stir until the mixture becomes significantly more solid and is hard to stir – this should take about 5–6 minutes.
2. Grease a 15 x 15-cm/6 x 6-in. baking pan with some of the olive oil. Tip the polenta into the baking pan, smoothing down with the back of a wet spoon. Leave to cool at room temperature for about 30 minutes, then pop into the fridge for at least an hour.
3. Remove the polenta from the fridge and carefully tip out onto a chopping board. Slice the polenta into fingers 7.5 x 1 x 2 cm/3 x ½ x ¾ in. Roll the polenta fingers in the flour, then spray or drizzle the remaining olive oil over the fingers.
4. Preheat the air-fryer to 200ºC/400ºF.
5. Lay the fingers apart from one another in a single layer in the preheated air-fryer (you may need to cook these in batches, depending on the size of your air-fryer). Air-fry for 9 minutes, turning once halfway through cooking. Serve immediately with garlic mayonnaise.

Crunchy Mexican Breakfast Wrap

Servings: 2
Cooking Time:xx
Ingredients:

- 2 large tortillas
- 2 corn tortillas
- 1 sliced jalapeño pepper
- 4 tbsp ranchero sauce
- 1 sliced avocado
- 25g cooked pinto beans

Directions:

1. Take each of your large tortillas and add the egg, jalapeño, sauce, the corn tortillas, the avocado and the pinto beans, in that order. If you want to add more sauce at this point, you can
2. Fold over your wrap to make sure that nothing escapes
3. Place each wrap into your fryer and cook at 190ºC for 6 minutes
4. Remove your wraps and place in the oven, cooking for a further 5 minutes at 180ºC, until crispy
5. Place each wrap into a frying pan and crisp a little more on a low heat, for a couple of minutes on each side

Tangy Breakfast Hash

Servings: 6
Cooking Time:xx
Ingredients:

- 2 tbsp olive oil
- 2 sweet potatoes, cut into cubes
- 1 tbsp smoked paprika
- 1 tsp salt
- 1 tsp black pepper
- 2 slices of bacon, cut into small pieces

Directions:

1. Preheat your air fryer to 200ºC
2. Pour the olive oil into a large mixing bowl
3. Add the bacon, seasonings, potatoes and toss to evenly coat
4. Transfer the mixture into the air fryer and cook for 12-16 minutes
5. Stir after 10 minutes and continue to stir periodically for another 5 minutes

Blueberry Bread

Servings: 8
Cooking Time:xx
Ingredients:

- 260ml milk
- 3 eggs
- 25g protein powder
- 400g frozen blueberries
- 600g bisquick or pancake mixture

Directions:

1. Take a large mixing bowl and combine all ingredients until smooth
2. Preheat the air fryer to 250ºC
3. Place the mixture into a loaf tin
4. Place the tin into the air fryer and cook for 30 minutes
5. A toothpick should come out clean if the bread is cooked

Patatas Bravas

Servings: 4
Cooking Time:xx
Ingredients:

- 300g potatoes
- 1 tsp garlic powder
- 1 tbsp avocado oil
- 1 tbsp smoked paprika
- Salt and pepper to taste

Directions:

1. Peel the potatoes and cut them into cubes
2. Bring a large saucepan of water to the boil and add the potatoes, cooking for 6 minutes
3. Strain the potatoes and place them on a piece of kitchen towel, allowing to dry
4. Take a large mixing bowl and add the garlic powder, salt, and pepper and add the avocado oil, mixing together well
5. Add the potatoes to the bowl and coat liberally
6. Place the potatoes into the basket and arrange them with space in-between
7. Set your fryer to 200ºC
8. Cook the potatoes for 15 minutes, giving them a shake at the halfway point
9. Remove and serve

Delicious Breakfast Casserole

Servings: 4
Cooking Time:xx

Ingredients:

- 4 frozen hash browns
- 8 sausages, cut into pieces
- 4 eggs
- 1 diced yellow pepper
- 1 diced green pepper
- 1 diced red pepper
- Half a diced onion

Directions:

1. Line the bottom of your fryer with aluminium foil and arrange the hash browns inside
2. Add the sausage on top (uncooked)
3. Now add the onions and the peppers, sprinkling evenly
4. Cook the casserole on 170ºC for around 10 minutes
5. Open your fryer and give the mixture a good stir
6. Combine the eggs in a small bowl and pour over the casserole, closing the lid
7. Cook for another 10 minutes on the same temperature
8. Serve with a little seasoning to taste

Hard Boiled Eggs Air Fryer Style

Servings: 2
Cooking Time:xx

Ingredients:

- 4 large eggs
- 1 tsp cayenne pepper
- Salt and pepper for seasoning

Directions:

1. Preheat the air fryer to 220ºC
2. Take a wire rack and place inside the air fryer
3. Lay the eggs on the rack
4. Cook for between 15-17 minutes, depending upon how you like your eggs
5. Remove from the fryer and place in a bowl of cold water for around 5 minutes
6. Peel and season with the cayenne and the salt and pepper

Cheesy Sausage Breakfast Pockets

Servings: 2
Cooking Time:xx

Ingredients:

- 1 packet of regular puff pastry
- 4 sausages, cooked and crumbled into pieces
- 5 eggs
- 50g cooked bacon
- 50g grated cheddar cheese

Directions:

1. Scramble your eggs in your usual way
2. Add the sausage and the bacon as you are cooking the eggs and combine well
3. Take your pastry sheets and cut rectangular shapes
4. Add a little of the egg and meat mixture to one half of each pastry piece
5. Fold the rectangles over and use a fork to seal down the edges
6. Place your pockets into your air fryer and cook at 190ºC for 10 minutes
7. Allow to cool before serving

Breakfast "pop Tarts"

Servings: 6
Cooking Time:xx

Ingredients:

- 2 slices of prepared pie crust, shortbread or filo will work fine
- 2 tbsp strawberry jam
- 60ml plain yogurt
- 1 tsp cornstarch
- 1 tsp Stevia sweetener
- 2 tbsp cream cheese
- A drizzle of olive oil

Directions:

1. Lay your pie crust flat and cut into 6 separate rectangular pieces
2. In a small bowl, mix together the cornstarch and the jam
3. Spread 1 tablespoon of the mixture on top of the crust
4. Fold each crust over to form the tart
5. Seal down the edges using a fork
6. Arrange your tarts inside the frying basket and spray with a little olive oil
7. Heat to 175ºC and cook for 10 minutes
8. Meanwhile, combine the yogurt, cream cheese and Stevia in a bowl
9. Remove the tarts and allow to cool
10. Once cool, add the frosting on top and sprinkle with the sugar sprinkles

French Toast

Servings: 2
Cooking Time:xx

Ingredients:

- 2 beaten eggs
- 2 tbsp softened butter
- 4 slices of sandwich bread
- 1 tsp cinnamon
- 1 tsp nutmeg
- 1 tsp ground cloves
- 1 tsp maple syrup

Directions:

1. Preheat your fryer to 180ºC
2. Take a bowl and add the eggs, salt, cinnamon, nutmeg, and cloves, combining well
3. Take your bread and butter each side, cutting into strips
4. Dip the bread slices into the egg mixture
5. Arrange each slice into the basket of your fryer
6. Cook for 2 minutes
7. Take the basket out and spray with a little cooking spray
8. Turn over the slices and place back into the fryer
9. Cook for 4 minutes
10. Remove and serve with maple syrup

Breakfast Sausage Burgers

Servings: 2
Cooking Time:xx

Ingredients:

- 8 links of your favourite sausage
- Salt and pepper to taste

Directions:

1. Remove the sausage from the skins and use a fork to create a smooth mixture
2. Season to your liking
3. Shape the sausage mixture into burgers or patties
4. Preheat your air fryer to 260ºC
5. Arrange the burgers in the fryer, so they are not touching each other
6. Cook for 8 minutes
7. Serve still warm

Wholegrain Pitta Chips

Servings: 2
Cooking Time:xx

Ingredients:

- 2 round wholegrain pittas, chopped into quarters
- 1 teaspoon olive oil
- ½ teaspoon garlic salt

Directions:

1. Preheat the air-fryer to 180ºC/350ºF.
2. Spray or brush each pitta quarter with olive oil and sprinkle with garlic salt. Place in the preheated air-fryer and air-fry for 4 minutes, turning halfway through cooking. Serve immediately.

Blanket Breakfast Eggs

Servings: 2
Cooking Time:xx

Ingredients:

- 2 eggs
- 2 slices of sandwich bread
- Olive oil spray
- Salt and pepper to taste

Directions:

1. Preheat your air fryer to 190ºC and spray with a little oil
2. Meanwhile, take your bread and cut a hole into the middle of each piece
3. Place one slice inside your fryer and crack one egg into the middle
4. Season with a little salt and pepper
5. Cook for 5 minutes, before turning over and cooking for a further 2 minutes
6. Remove the first slice and repeat the process with the remaining slice of bread and egg

Plantain Fries

Servings: 2
Cooking Time:xx
Ingredients:

- 1 ripe plantain (yellow and brown outside skin)
- 1 teaspoon olive oil
- ¼ teaspoon salt

Directions:

1. Preheat the air-fryer to 180ºC/350ºF.
2. Peel the plantain and slice into fries about 6 x 1 cm/2½ x ½ in. Toss the fries in oil and salt, making sure every fry is coated.
3. Tip into the preheated air-fryer in a single layer (you may need to cook them in two batches, depending on the size of your air-fryer) and air-fry for 13–14 minutes until brown on the outside and soft on the inside. Serve immediately.

Healthy Breakfast Bagels

Servings: 2
Cooking Time:xx
Ingredients:

- 170g self raising flour
- 120ml plain yogurt
- 1 egg

Directions:

1. Take a large mixing bowl, combine the flour and the yogurt to create a dough
2. Cover a flat surface with a little extra flour and set the dough down
3. Create four separate and even balls
4. Roll each ball out into a rope shape and form a bagel with each
5. Take a small mixing bowl and whisk the egg
6. Brush the egg over the top of the bagel
7. Arrange the bagels inside your fryer evenly
8. Cook at 170ºC for 10 minutes
9. Allow to cool before serving

Whole Mini Peppers

Servings: 2
Cooking Time:xx
Ingredients:

- 9 whole mini (bell) peppers
- 1 teaspoon olive oil
- ¼ teaspoon salt

Directions:

1. Preheat the air-fryer to 180ºC/350ºF.
2. Place the peppers in a baking dish that fits in for your air-fryer and drizzle over the oil, then sprinkle over the salt.
3. Add the dish to the preheated air-fryer and air-fry for 10–12 minutes, depending on how 'chargrilled' you like your peppers.

Avocado Fries

Servings: 2
Cooking Time:xx

Ingredients:

- 35 g/¼ cup plain/all-purpose flour (gluten free if you wish)
- ½ teaspoon chilli/chili powder
- 1 egg, beaten
- 50 g/heaped ½ cup dried breadcrumbs (gluten-free if you wish; see page 9)
- 1 avocado, skin and stone removed, and each half sliced lengthways
- salt and freshly ground black pepper

Directions:

1. Preheat the air-fryer to 200ºC/400ºF.
2. In a bowl combine the flour and chilli/chili powder, then season with salt and pepper. Place the beaten egg in a second bowl and the breadcrumbs in a third bowl.
3. Dip each avocado slice in the seasoned flour (shaking off any excess), then the egg and finally the breadcrumbs.
4. Add the breaded avocado slices to the preheated air-fryer and air-fry for 6 minutes, turning after 4 minutes. Serve immediately.

Potato & Chorizo Frittata

Servings: 2
Cooking Time:xx

Ingredients:

- 3 eggs
- 1 sliced chorizo sausage
- 1 potato, boiled and cubed
- 50g feta cheese
- 50g frozen sweetcorn
- A pinch of salt
- 1 tbsp olive oil

Directions:

1. Add a little olive oil to the frying basket
2. Add the corn, potato, and sliced chorizo to the basket
3. Cook at 180ºC until the sausage is a little brown
4. In a small bowl, beat together the eggs with a little seasoning
5. Pour the eggs into the pan
6. Crumble the feta on top
7. Cook for 5 minutes
8. Remove and serve in slices

Blueberry & Lemon Breakfast Muffins

Servings: 12
Cooking Time:xx
Ingredients:

- 315g self raising flour
- 65g sugar
- 120ml double cream
- 2 tbsp of light cooking oil
- 2 eggs
- 125g blueberries
- The zest and juice of a lemon
- 1 tsp vanilla

Directions:

1. Take a small bowl and mix the self raising flour and sugar together
2. Take another bowl and mix together the oil, juice, eggs, cream, and vanilla
3. Add this mixture to the flour mixture and blend together
4. Add the blueberries and fold
5. You will need individual muffin holders, silicone works best. Spoon the mixture into the holders
6. Cook at 150ºC for 10 minutes
7. Check at the halfway point to check they're not cooking too fast
8. Remove and allow to cool

Monte Cristo Breakfast Sandwich

Servings: 4
Cooking Time:xx
Ingredients:

- 1 egg
- 2 slices of sandwich bread
- 1/4 tsp vanilla extract
- 4 slices of sliced Swiss cheese
- 4 slices of sliced deli ham
- 4 slices of sliced turkey
- 1 tsp melted butter
- Powdered sugar for serving

Directions:

1. In a small bowl, mix together the egg and vanilla extract, combining well
2. Take your bread and assemble your sandwich, starting with a slice of cheese, then the ham, turkey, and then another slice of the cheese, with the other slice of bread on the top
3. Compress the sandwich a little, so it cooks better
4. Take a piece of cooking foil and brush over it with the butter
5. Take your sandwich and dip each side into the egg mixture, leaving it to one side for around half a minute
6. Place the sandwich on the foil and place it inside your fryer
7. Cook at 200ºC for around 10 minutes, before turning the sandwich over and cooking for another 8 minutes
8. Transfer your sandwich onto a plate and sprinkle with a little powdered sugar

Potato Fries

Servings: 2
Cooking Time:xx

Ingredients:

- 2 large potatoes (baking potato size)
- 1 teaspoon olive oil
- salt

Directions:

1. Peel the potatoes and slice into fries about 5 x 1.5cm/¾ x ¾ in. by the length of the potato. Submerge the fries in a bowl of cold water and place in the fridge for about 10 minutes.
2. Meanwhile, preheat the air-fryer to 160ºC/325ºF.
3. Drain the fries thoroughly, then toss in the oil and season. Tip into the preheated air-fryer in a single layer (you may need to cook them in two batches, depending on the size of your air-fryer). Air-fry for 15 minutes, tossing once during cooking by shaking the air-fryer drawer, then increase the temperature of the air-fryer to 200ºC/400ºF and cook for a further 3 minutes. Serve immediately.

Toad In The Hole, Breakfast Style

Servings: 4
Cooking Time:xx

Ingredients:

- 1 sheet of puff pastry (defrosted)
- 4 eggs
- 4 tbsp grated cheese (cheddar works well)
- 4 slices of cooked ham, cut into pieces
- Chopped fresh herbs of your choice

Directions:

1. Preheat your air fryer to 200ºC
2. Take your pastry sheet and place it on a flat surface, cutting it into four pieces
3. Take two of the pastry sheets and place them inside your fryer, cooking for up to 8 minutes, until done
4. Remove the pastry and flatten the centre down with a spoon, to form a deep hole
5. Add a tablespoon of the cheese and a tablespoon of the ham into the hole
6. Crack one egg into the hole
7. Return the pastry to the air fryer and cook for another 6 minutes, or until the egg is done as you like it
8. Remove and allow to cool
9. Repeat the process with the rest of the pastry remaining
10. Sprinkle fresh herbs on top and serve

Sauces & Snack And Appetiser Recipes

Spicy Peanuts

Servings: 8
Cooking Time:xx
Ingredients:

- 2 tbsp olive oil
- 3 tbsp seafood seasoning
- ½ tsp cayenne
- 300g raw peanuts
- Salt to taste

Directions:

1. Preheat the air fryer to 160ºC
2. Whisk together ingredients in a bowl and stir in the peanuts
3. Add to air fryer and cook for 10 minutes, shake then cook for a further 10 minutes
4. Sprinkle with salt and cook for another 5 minutes

Potato Patties

Servings: 12
Cooking Time:xx
Ingredients:

- 150g instant mash
- 50g peas and carrots
- 2 tbsp coriander
- 1 tbsp oil
- 100ml hot water
- ½ tsp turmeric
- ½ tsp cayenne
- ½ tsp salt
- ½ tsp cumin seeds
- ¼ tsp ground cumin

Directions:

1. Place all the ingredients in a bowl. Mix well cover and stand for 10 minutes
2. Preheat the air fryer to 200ºC
3. Spray the air fryer with cooking spray
4. Make 12 patties, place in the air fryer and cook for 10 minutes

Beetroot Crisps

Servings: 2
Cooking Time:xx
Ingredients:

- 3 medium beetroots
- 2 tbsp oil
- Salt to taste

Directions:

1. Peel and thinly slice the beetroot
2. Coat with the oil and season with salt
3. Preheat the air fryer to 200ºC
4. Place in the air fryer and cook for 12-18 minutes until crispy

Korean Chicken Wings

Servings: 2
Cooking Time:xx
Ingredients:

- 25ml soy sauce
- 40g brown sugar
- 2 tbsp hot pepper paste
- 1 tsp sesame oil
- ½ tsp ginger paste
- ½ tsp garlic paste
- 2 green onions, chopped
- 400g chicken wings
- 1 tbsp vegetable oil

Directions:

1. Preheat air fryer to 200ºC
2. Place all ingredients apart from chicken wings and vegetable oil in a pan and simmer for about 4 minutes set aside
3. Massage the vegetable oil into the chicken wings
4. Place in the air fryer and cook for about 10 minutes
5. Turn and cook for a further 10 minutes
6. Coat the wings in the sauce and return to the air fryer
7. Cook for about 2 minutes

Salt And Vinegar Chickpeas

Servings: 5
Cooking Time:xx
Ingredients:

- 1 can chickpeas
- 100ml white vinegar
- 1 tbsp olive oil
- Salt to taste

Directions:

1. Combine chickpeas and vinegar in a pan, simmer remove from heat and stand for 30 minutes
2. Preheat the air fryer to 190ºC
3. Drain chickpeas
4. Place chickpeas in the air fryer and cook for about 4 minutes
5. Pour chickpeas into an ovenproof bowl drizzle with oil, sprinkle with salt
6. Place bowl in the air fryer and cook for another 4 minutes

Pretzel Bites

Servings: 2

Cooking Time:xx

Ingredients:

- 650g flour
- 2.5 tsp active dry yeast
- 260ml hot water
- 1 tsp salt
- 4 tbsp melted butter
- 2 tbsp sugar

Directions:

1. Take a large bowl and add the flour, sugar and salt
2. Take another bowl and combine the hot water and yeast, stirring until the yeast has dissolved
3. Then, add the yeast mixture to the flour mixture and use your hands to combine
4. Knead for 2 minutes
5. Cover the bowl with a kitchen towel for around half an hour
6. Divide the dough into 6 pieces
7. Preheat the air fryer to 260ºC
8. Take each section of dough and tear off a piece, rolling it in your hands to create a rope shape, that is around 1" in thickness
9. Cut into 2" strips
10. Place the small dough balls into the air fryer and leave a little space in-between
11. Cook for 6 minutes
12. Once cooked, remove and brush with melted butter and sprinkle salt on top

Waffle Fries

Servings: 4

Cooking Time:xx

Ingredients:

- 2 large potatoes, russet potatoes work best
- 1 tsp salt for seasoning
- Waffle cutter

Directions:

1. Peel the potatoes and slice using the waffle cutter. You can also use a mandolin cutter that has a blade
2. Transfer the potatoes to a bowl and season with the salt, coating evenly
3. Add to the air fryer and cook at 220ºC for 15 minutes, shaking every so often

Spicy Chickpeas

Servings: 4

Cooking Time:xx

Ingredients:

- 1 can chickpeas
- 1 tbsp yeast
- 1 tbsp olive oil
- 1 tsp paprika
- 1 tsp garlic powder
- ½ tsp salt
- Pinch cumin

Directions:

1. Preheat air fryer to 180ºC
2. Combine all ingredients
3. Add to the air fryer and cook for 22 minutes tossing every 4 minutes until cooked

Snack Style Falafel

Servings: 15
Cooking Time:xx

Ingredients:

- 150g dry garbanzo beans
- 300g coriander
- 75g flat leaf parsley
- 1 red onion, quartered
- 1 clove garlic
- 2 tbsp chickpea flour
- Cooking spray
- 1 tbsp cumin
- 1 tbsp coriander
- 1 tbsp sriracha
- ½ tsp baking powder
- Salt and pepper to taste
- ¼ tsp baking soda

Directions:

1. Add all ingredients apart from the baking soda and baking powder to a food processor and blend well
2. Cover and rest for 1 hour
3. Heat air fryer to 190ºC
4. Add baking powder and baking soda to mix and combine
5. Form mix into 15 equal balls
6. Spray air fryer with cooking spray
7. Add to air fryer and cook for 8-10 minutes

Tasty Pumpkin Seeds

Servings: 2
Cooking Time:xx

Ingredients:

- 1 ¾ cups pumpkin seeds
- 2 tsp avocado oil
- 1 tsp paprika
- 1 tsp salt

Directions:

1. Preheat air fryer to 180ºC
2. Add all ingredients to a bowl and mix well
3. Place in the air fryer and cook for 35 minutes shaking frequently

Popcorn Tofu

Servings: 4
Cooking Time:xx

Ingredients:

- 400g firm tofu
- 100g chickpea flour
- 100g oatmeal
- 2 tbsp yeast
- 150ml milk
- 400g breadcrumbs
- 1 tsp garlic powder
- 1 tsp onion powder
- 1 tbsp dijon mustard
- ½ tsp salt
- ½ tsp pepper
- 2 tbsp vegetable bouillon

Directions:

1. Rip the tofu into pieces. Place the breadcrumbs into a bowl, in another bowl mix the remaining ingredients
2. Dip the tofu into the batter mix and then dip into the breadcrumbs
3. Heat the air fryer to 175ºC
4. Place the tofu in the air fryer and cook for 12 minutes shaking halfway through

Jalapeño Poppers

Servings: 2

Cooking Time:xx

Ingredients:

- 10 jalapeños, halved and deseeded
- 100g cream cheese
- 50g parsley
- 150g breadcrumbs

Directions:

1. Mix 1/2 the breadcrumbs with the cream cheese
2. Add the parsley
3. Stuff the peppers with the cream cheese mix
4. Top the peppers with the remaining breadcrumbs
5. Heat the air fryer to 185ºC
6. Place in the air fryer and cook for 6-8 minutes

Pork Jerky

Servings: 35

Cooking Time:xx

Ingredients:

- 300g mince pork
- 1 tbsp oil
- 1 tbsp sriracha
- 1 tbsp soy
- ½ tsp pink curing salt
- 1 tbsp rice vinegar
- ½ tsp salt
- ½ tsp pepper
- ½ tsp onion powder

Directions:

1. Mix all ingredients in a bowl until combined
2. Refrigerate for about 8 hours
3. Shape into sticks and place in the air fryer
4. Heat the air fryer to 160ºC
5. Cook for 1 hour turn then cook for another hour
6. Turn again and cook for another hour
7. Cover with paper and sit for 8 hours

Chicken & Bacon Parcels

Servings: 4

Cooking Time:xx

Ingredients:

- 2 chicken breasts, boneless and skinless
- 200ml BBQ sauce
- 7 slices of bacon, cut lengthwise into halves
- 2 tbsp brown sugar

Directions:

1. Preheat the air fryer to 220ºC
2. Cut the chicken into strips, you should have 7 in total
3. Wrap two strips of the bacon around each piece of chicken
4. Brush the BBQ sauce over the top and sprinkle with the brown sugar
5. Place the chicken into the basket and cook for 5 minutes
6. Turn the chicken over and cook for another 5 minutes

Mozzarella Sticks

Servings: 4
Cooking Time:xx

Ingredients:

- 60ml water
- 50g flour
- 5 tbsp cornstarch
- 1 tbsp cornmeal
- 1 tsp garlic powder
- ½ tsp salt
- 100g breadcrumbs
- ½ tsp pepper
- ½ tsp parsley
- ½ tsp onion powder
- ¼ tsp oregano
- ½ tsp basil
- 200g mozzarella cut into ½ inch strips

Directions:

1. Mix water, flour, cornstarch, cornmeal, garlic powder and salt in a bowl
2. Stir breadcrumbs, pepper, parsley, onion powder, oregano and basil together in another bowl
3. Dip the mozzarella sticks in the batter then coat in the breadcrumbs
4. Heat the air fryer to 200ºC
5. Cook for 6 minutes turn and cook for another 6 minutes

Lumpia

Servings: 16
Cooking Time:xx

Ingredients:

- 400g Italian sausage
- 1 sliced onion
- 1 chopped carrot
- 50g chopped water chestnuts
- Cooking spray
- 2 cloves minced, garlic
- 2 tbsp soy sauce
- ½ tsp salt
- ¼ tsp ground ginger
- 16 spring roll wrappers

Directions:

1. Cook sausage in a pan for about 5 minutes. Add green onions, onions, water chestnuts and carrot cook for 7 minutes
2. Add garlic and cook for a further 2 minutes
3. Add the soy sauce, salt and ginger, stir to mix well
4. Add filling to each spring roll wrapper.
5. Roll over the bottom and tuck in the sides, continue to roll up the spring roll
6. Spray with cooking spray and place in the air fryer
7. Cook at 200ºC for 4 minutes turn and cook for a further 4 minutes

Cheese Wontons

Servings: 8

Cooking Time:xx

Ingredients:

- 8 wonton wrappers
- 1 carton pimento cheese
- Small dish of water
- Cooking spray

Directions:

1. Place one tsp of cheese in the middle of each wonton wrapper
2. Brush the edges of each wonton wrapper with water
3. Fold over to create a triangle and seal
4. Heat the air fryer to 190ºC
5. Spray the wontons with cooking spray
6. Place in the air fryer and cook for 3 minutes
7. Turnover and cook for a further 3 minutes

Salt And Vinegar Chips

Servings: 4

Cooking Time:xx

Ingredients:

- 6-10 Jerusalem artichokes, thinly sliced
- 150ml apple cider vinegar
- 2 tbsp olive oil
- Sea salt

Directions:

1. Soak the artichoke in apple cider vinegar for 20-30 minutes
2. Preheat the air fryer to 200ºC
3. Coat the artichoke in olive oil
4. Place in the air fryer and cook for 15 Minutes
5. Sprinkle with salt

Tostones

Servings: 4

Cooking Time:xx

Ingredients:

- 2 unripe plantains
- Olive oil cooking spray
- 300ml of water
- Salt to taste

Directions:

1. Preheat the air fryer to 200ºC
2. Slice the tips off the plantain
3. Cut the plantain into 1 inch chunks
4. Place in the air fryer spray with oil and cook for 5 minutes
5. Remove the plantain from the air fryer and smash to ½ inch pieces
6. Soak in a bowl of salted water
7. Remove from the water and return to the air fryer season with salt cook for 5 minutes
8. Turn and cook for another 5 minutes

Focaccia Bread

Servings: 8
Cooking Time:xx

Ingredients:

- 500g pizza dough
- 3 tbsp olive oil
- 2-3 garlic cloves, chopped
- ¼ tsp red pepper flakes
- 50g parsley
- 1 tsp basil
- 100g chopped red peppers
- 60g black olives halved
- 60g green olives halved
- Salt and pepper to taste

Directions:

1. Preheat the air fryer to 180ºC, make indentations in the pizza dough with your finger tips and set aside
2. Heat the olive oil in a pan add the garlic and cook for a few minutes, add the remaining ingredients and cook for another 5-8 minutes not letting the oil get too hot
3. Spread the oil mix over the dough with a spatula
4. Place in the air fryer and cook for 12-15 minutes

Pasta Chips

Servings: 2
Cooking Time:xx

Ingredients:

- 300g dry pasta bows
- 1 tbsp olive oil
- 1 tbsp nutritional yeast
- 1½ tsp Italian seasoning
- ½ tsp salt

Directions:

1. Cook the pasta for half the time stated on the packet
2. Drain and mix with the oil, yeast, seasoning and salt
3. Place in the air fryer and cook at 200ºC for 5 minutes shake and cook for a further 3 minutes until crunchy

Tortellini Bites

Servings: 6
Cooking Time:xx

Ingredients:

- 200g cheese tortellini
- 150g flour
- 100g panko bread crumbs
- 50g grated parmesan
- 1 tsp dried oregano
- 2 eggs
- ½ tsp garlic powder
- ½ tsp chilli flakes
- Salt
- Pepper

Directions:

1. Cook the tortellini according to the packet instructions
2. Mix the panko, parmesan, oregano, garlic powder, chilli flakes salt and pepper in a bowl
3. Beat the eggs in another bowl and place the flour in a third bowl
4. Coat the tortellini in flour, then egg and then in the panko mix
5. Place in the air fryer and cook at 185ºC for 10 minutes until crispy
6. Serve with marinara sauce for dipping

Poultry Recipes

Cornflake Chicken Nuggets

Servings: 4
Cooking Time:xx
Ingredients:

- 100 g/4 cups cornflakes (gluten-free if you wish)
- 70 g/½ cup plus ½ tablespoon plain/all-purpose flour (gluten-free if you wish)
- 2 eggs, beaten
- ½ teaspoon salt
- ¼ teaspoon freshly ground black pepper
- 600 g/1 lb. 5 oz. mini chicken fillets

Directions:

1. Grind the cornflakes in a food processor to a crumb-like texture. Place the flour in one bowl and the beaten eggs in a second bowl; season both bowls with the salt and pepper. Coat each chicken fillet in flour, tapping off any excess. Next dip each flour-coated chicken fillet into the egg, then the cornflakes until fully coated.
2. Preheat the air-fryer to 180ºC/350ºF.
3. Add the chicken fillets to the preheated air-fryer (you may need to add the fillets in two batches, depending on the size of your air-fryer) and air-fry for 10 minutes, turning halfway through cooking. Check the internal temperature of the nuggets has reached at least 74ºC/165ºF using a meat thermometer – if not, cook for another few minutes and then serve.
4. VARIATION: SIMPLE CHICKEN NUGGETS
5. For a simpler version, replace the crushed cornflakes with 90 g/1¼ cups dried breadcrumbs (see page 9). Prepare and air-fry in the same way.

Air Fryer Chicken Thigh Schnitzel

Servings: 4
Cooking Time:xx
Ingredients:

- 300g boneless chicken thighs
- 160g seasoned breadcrumbs
- 1 tsp salt
- ½ tsp ground black pepper
- 30g flour
- 1 egg
- Cooking spray

Directions:

1. Lay the chicken on a sheet of parchment paper and add another on top
2. Use a mallet or a rolling pin to flatten it down
3. Take a bowl and add the breadcrumbs with the salt and pepper
4. Place the flour into another bowl
5. Dip the chicken into the flour, then the egg, and then the breadcrumbs
6. Preheat air fryer to 190ºC
7. Place the chicken into the air fryer and spray with cooking oil
8. Cook for 6 minutes

Crunchy Chicken Tenders

Servings: 4
Cooking Time:xx

Ingredients:

- 8 regular chicken tenders (frozen work best)
- 1 egg
- 2 tbsp olive oil
- 150g dried breadcrumbs

Directions:

1. Heat the fryer to 175ºC
2. In a small bowl, beat the egg
3. In another bowl, combine the oil and the breadcrumbs together
4. Take one tender and first dip it into the egg, and then cover it in the breadcrumb mixture
5. Place the tender into the fryer basket
6. Repeat with the rest of the tenders, arranging them carefully so they don't touch inside the basket
7. Cook for 12 minutes, checking that they are white in the centre before serving

Buttermilk Chicken

Servings: 4
Cooking Time:xx

Ingredients:

- 500g chicken thighs, skinless and boneless
- 180ml buttermilk
- 40g tapioca flour
- ½ tsp garlic salt
- 1 egg
- 75g all purpose flour
- ½ tsp brown sugar
- 1 tsp garlic powder
- ½ tsp paprika
- ½ tsp onion powder
- ¼ tsp oregano
- Salt and pepper to taste

Directions:

1. Take a medium mixing bowl and combine the buttermilk and hot sauce
2. Add the tapioca flour, garlic salt and black pepper in a plastic bag and shake
3. Beat the egg
4. Take the chicken thighs and tip into the buttermilk, then the tapioca mixture, the egg, and then the flour
5. Preheat air fryer to 190ºC
6. Cook the chicken thighs for 10 minutes, until white in the middle

Chicken Tikka

Servings: 2
Cooking Time:xx

Ingredients:

- 2 chicken breasts, diced
- FIRST MARINADE
- freshly squeezed juice of ½ a lemon
- 1 tablespoon freshly grated ginger
- 1 tablespoon freshly grated garlic
- a good pinch of salt
- SECOND MARINADE
- 100 g/½ cup Greek yogurt
- ½ teaspoon chilli powder
- ½ teaspoon chilli paste
- ½ teaspoon turmeric
- ½ teaspoon garam masala
- 1 tablespoon olive oil

Directions:

1. Mix the ingredients for the first marinade together in a bowl, add in the chicken and stir to coat all the chicken pieces. Leave in the fridge to marinate for 20 minutes.
2. Combine the second marinade ingredients. Once the first marinade has had 20 minutes, add the second marinade to the chicken and stir well. Leave in the fridge for at least 4 hours.
3. Preheat the air-fryer to 180ºC/350ºF.
4. Thread the chicken pieces onto metal skewers that fit in your air-fryer. Add the skewers to the preheated air-fryer and air-fry for 10 minutes. Check the internal temperature of the chicken has reached at least 74ºC/165ºF using a meat thermometer – if not, cook for another few minutes and then serve.

Turkey Cutlets In Mushroom Sauce

Servings: 2
Cooking Time:xx

Ingredients:

- 2 turkey cutlets
- 1 tbsp butter
- 1 can of cream of mushroom sauce
- 160ml milk
- Salt and pepper for seasoning

Directions:

1. Preheat the air fryer to 220ºC
2. Brush the turkey cults with the butter and seasoning
3. Place in the air fryer and cook for 11 minutes
4. Add the mushroom soup and milk to a pan and cook over the stone for around 10 minutes, stirring every so often
5. Top the turkey cutlets with the sauce

Thai Turkey Burgers

Servings: 4
Cooking Time:xx

Ingredients:

- 1 courgette/zucchini, about 200 g/7 oz.
- 400 g/14 oz. minced/ground turkey breast
- 35 g/½ cup fresh breadcrumbs (gluten-free if you wish)
- 1 teaspoon Thai 7 spice seasoning
- 1 teaspoon salt
- 1 teaspoon olive oil

Directions:

1. Coarsely grate the courgette/zucchini, then place in a piece of muslin/cheesecloth and squeeze out the water. Combine the grated courgette with all other ingredients except the olive oil, mixing together well. Divide the mixture into 4 equal portions and mould into burgers. Brush with oil.
2. Preheat the air-fryer to 190°C/375°C.
3. Add the turkey burgers to the preheated air-fryer and air-fry for 15 minutes, turning once halfway through cooking. Check the internal temperature of the burgers has reached at least 74°C/165°F using a meat thermometer – if not, cook for another few minutes and then serve.

Nashville Chicken

Servings: 4
Cooking Time:xx

Ingredients:

- 400g boneless chicken breast tenders
- 2 tsp salt
- 2 tsp coarsely ground black pepper
- 2 tbsp hot sauce
- 2 tbsp pickle juice
- 500g all purpose flour
- 3 large eggs
- 300ml buttermilk
- 2 tbsp olive oil
- 6 tbsp cayenne pepper
- 3 tbsp dark brown sugar
- 1 tsp chilli powder
- 1 tsp garlic powder
- 1 tsp paprika
- Salt and pepper to taste

Directions:

1. Take a large mixing bowl and add the chicken, hot sauce, pickle juice, salt and pepper and combine
2. Place in the refrigerator for 3 hours
3. Transfer the flour to a bowl
4. Take another bowl and add the eggs, buttermilk and 1 tbsp of the hot sauce, combining well
5. Press each piece of chicken into the flour and coat well
6. Place the chicken into the buttermilk mixture and then back into the flour
7. Allow to sit or 10 minutes
8. Preheat the air fryer to 193C
9. Whisk together the spices, brown sugar and olive oil to make the sauce and pour over the chicken tenders
10. Serve whilst still warm

Buffalo Wings

Servings: 4
Cooking Time:xx

Ingredients:

- 500g chicken wings
- 1 tbsp olive oil
- 5 tbsp cayenne pepper sauce
- 75g butter
- 2 tbsp vinegar
- 1 tsp garlic powder
- ¼ tsp cayenne pepper

Directions:

1. Preheat the air fryer to 182C
2. Take a large mixing bowl and add the chicken wings
3. Drizzle oil over the wings, coating evenly
4. Cook for 25 minutes and then flip the wings and cook for 5 more minutes
5. In a saucepan over a medium heat, mix the hot pepper sauce, butter, vinegar, garlic powder and cayenne pepper, combining well
6. Pour the sauce over the wings and flip to coat, before serving

Bbq Chicken Tenders

Servings: 6
Cooking Time:xx

Ingredients:

- 300g barbecue flavoured pork rinds
- 200g all purpose flour
- 1 tbsp barbecue seasoning
- 1 egg
- 400g chicken breast tenderloins
- Cooking spray

Directions:

1. Preheat the air fryer to 190ºC
2. Place the pork rinds into a food processor and blitz to a breadcrumb consistency, before transferring to a bowl
3. In a separate bowl, combine the flour and barbecue seasoning
4. Beat the egg in a small bowl
5. Take the chicken and first dip into the egg, then the flour, and then the breadcrumbs
6. Place the chicken into the air fryer and spray with cooking spray and cook for about 15 minutes

Cheddar & Bbq Stuffed Chicken

Servings: 2
Cooking Time:xx

Ingredients:

- 3 strips of bacon
- 100g cheddar cheese
- 3 tbsp barbecue sauce
- 300g skinless and boneless chicken breasts
- salt and ground pepper to taste

Directions:

1. Preheat the air fryer to 190ºC
2. Cook one of the back strips for 2 minutes, before cutting into small pieces
3. Increase the temperature of the air fryer to 200ºC
4. Mix together the cooked bacon, cheddar cheese and 1 tbsp barbecue sauce
5. Take the chicken and make a pouch by cutting a 1 inch gap into the top
6. Stuff the pouch with the bacon and cheese mixture and then wrap around the chicken breast
7. Coat the chicken with the rest of the BBQ sauce
8. Cook for 10 minutes in the air fryer, before turning and cooking for an additional 10 minutes

Honey Cajun Chicken Thighs

Servings: 6
Cooking Time:xx

Ingredients:

- 100ml buttermilk
- 1 tsp hot sauce
- 400g skinless, boneless chicken thighs
- 150g all purpose flour
- 60g tapioca flour
- 2.5 tsp cajun seasoning
- ½ tsp garlic salt
- ½ tsp honey powder
- ¼ tsp ground paprika
- ⅛ tsp cayenne pepper
- 4 tsp honey

Directions:

1. Take a large bowl and combine the buttermilk and hot sauce
2. Transfer to a plastic bag and add the chicken thighs
3. Allow to marinate for 30 minutes
4. Take another bowl and add the flour, tapioca flour, cajun seasoning, garlic, salt, honey powder, paprika, and cayenne pepper, combining well
5. Dredge the chicken through the mixture
6. Preheat the air fryer to 175C
7. Cook for 15 minutes before flipping the thighs over and cooking for another 10 minutes
8. Drizzle 1 tsp of honey over each thigh

Chicken And Cheese Chimichangas

Servings: 6

Cooking Time:xx

Ingredients:

- 100g shredded chicken (cooked)
- 150g nacho cheese
- 1 chopped jalapeño pepper
- 6 flour tortillas
- 5 tbsp salsa
- 60g refried beans
- 1 tsp cumin
- 0.5 tsp chill powder
- Salt and pepper to taste

Directions:

1. Take a large mixing bowl and add all of the ingredients, combining well
2. Add ⅓ of the filling to each tortilla and roll into a burrito shape
3. Spray the air fryer with cooking spray and heat to 200ºC
4. Place the chimichangas in the air fryer and cook for 7 minutes

Hawaiian Chicken

Servings: 2

Cooking Time:xx

Ingredients:

- 2 chicken breasts
- 1 tbsp butter
- A pinch of salt and pepper
- 160ml pineapple juice
- 25g brown sugar
- 3 tbsp soy sauce
- 2 tsp water
- 1 clove of garlic, minced
- 1 tsp grated ginger
- 2 tsp cornstarch

Directions:

1. Preheat the air fryer to 260ºC
2. Take a bowl and combine the butter and salt and pepper
3. Cover the chicken with the butter and cook in the fryer for 15 minutes, turning halfway
4. Remove and allow to rest for 5 minutes
5. Take another bowl and mix together the pineapple juice, soy sauce, garlic, ginger, and brown sugar
6. Transfer to a saucepan and simmer for 5 minutes
7. Combine the water and cornstarch and add to the sauce, stirring continually for another minute
8. Slice the chicken into strips and pour the sauce over the top

Orange Chicken

Servings: 2
Cooking Time:xx

Ingredients:

- 600g chicken thighs, boneless and skinless
- 2 tbsp cornstarch
- 60ml orange juice
- 1 tbsp soy sauce
- 2 tbsp brown sugar
- 1 tbsp rice wine vinegar
- 1/4 teaspoon ground ginger
- Pinch of red pepper flakes
- Zest of one orange
- 2 tsp water and 2 tsp cornstarch mixed together

Directions:

1. Preheat your air fryer to 250ºC
2. Take a bowl and combine the chicken with the cornstarch
3. Place in the air fryer and cook for 9 minutes
4. Take a bowl and combine the rest of the ingredients, except for the water and cornstarch mixture
5. Place in a saucepan and bring to the boil and then turn down to a simmer for 5 minutes
6. Add the water and cornstarch mixture to the pan and combine well
7. Remove the chicken from the fryer and pour the sauce over the top

Chicken And Wheat Stir Fry

Servings: 4
Cooking Time:xx

Ingredients:

- 1 onion
- 1 clove of garlic
- 200g skinless boneless chicken breast halves
- 3 whole tomatoes
- 400ml water
- 1 chicken stock cube
- 1 tbsp curry powder
- 130g wheat berries
- 1 tbsp vegetable oil

Directions:

1. Thinly slice the onion and garlic
2. Chop the chicken and tomatoes into cubes
3. Take a large saucepan and add the water, chicken stock, curry powder and wheat berries, combining well
4. Pour the oil into the air fryer bowl and heat for 5 minutes at 200ºC
5. Add the remaining ingredients and pour the contents into the air fryer
6. Cook for 15 minutes

Chicken Tikka Masala

Servings: 4

Cooking Time:xx

Ingredients:

- 100g tikka masala curry pasta
- 200g low fat yogurt
- 600g skinless chicken breasts
- 1 tbsp vegetable oil
- 1 onion, chopped
- 400g can of the whole, peeled tomatoes
- 20ml water
- 1 tbsp sugar
- 2 tbsp lemon juice
- 1 small bunch of chopped coriander leaves

Directions:

1. Take a bowl and combine the tikka masala curry paste with half the yogurt
2. Cut the chicken into strips
3. Preheat the air fryer to 200ºC
4. Add the yogurt mixture and coat the chicken until fully covered
5. Place into the refrigerator for 2 hours
6. Place the oil and onion in the air fryer and cook for 10 minutes
7. Add the marinated chicken, tomatoes, water and the rest of the yogurt and combine
8. Add the sugar and lemon juice and combine again
9. Cook for 15 minutes

Chicken & Potatoes

Servings: 4

Cooking Time:xx

Ingredients:

- 2 tbsp olive oil
- 2 potatoes, cut into 2" pieces
- 2 chicken breasts, cut into pieces of around 1" size
- 4 crushed garlic cloves
- 2 tsp smoked paprika
- 1 tsp thyme
- 1/2 tsp red chilli flakes
- Salt and pepper to taste

Directions:

1. Preheat your air fryer to 260ºC
2. Take a large bowl and combine the potatoes with half of the garlic, half the paprika, half the chilli flakes, salt, pepper and half the oil
3. Place into the air fryer and cook for 5 minutes, before turning over and cooking for another 5 minutes
4. Take a bowl and add the chicken with the rest of the seasonings and oil, until totally coated
5. Add the chicken to the potatoes mixture, moving the potatoes to the side
6. Cook for 10 minutes, turning the chicken halfway through

Quick Chicken Nuggets

Servings: 4
Cooking Time:xx

Ingredients:

- 500g chicken tenders
- 25g ranch salad dressing mixture
- 2 tbsp plain flour
- 100g breadcrumbs
- 1 egg, beaten
- Olive oil spray

Directions:

1. Take a large mixing bowl and arrange the chicken inside
2. Sprinkle the seasoning over the top and ensure the chicken is evenly coated
3. Place the chicken to one side for around 10 minutes
4. Add the flour into a resealable bag
5. Crack the egg into a small mixing bowl and whisk
6. Pour the breadcrumbs onto a medium sized plate
7. Transfer the chicken into the resealable bag and coat with the flour, giving it a good shake
8. Remove the chicken and dip into the egg, and then rolling it into the breadcrumbs, coating evenly
9. Repeat with all pieces of the chicken
10. Heat your air fryer to 200ºC
11. Arrange the chicken inside the fryer and add a little olive oil spray to avoid sticking
12. Cook for 4 minutes, before turning over and cooking for another 4 minutes
13. Remove and serve whilst hot

Pepper & Lemon Chicken Wings

Servings: 2
Cooking Time:xx

Ingredients:

- 1kg chicken wings
- 1/4 tsp cayenne pepper
- 2 tsp lemon pepper seasoning
- 3 tbsp butter
- 1 tsp honey
- An extra 1 tsp lemon pepper seasoning for the sauce

Directions:

1. Preheat the air fryer to 260ºC
2. Place the lemon pepper seasoning and cayenne in a bowl and combine
3. Coat the chicken in the seasoning
4. Place the chicken in the air fryer and cook for 20 minutes, turning over halfway
5. Turn the temperature up to 300ºC and cook for another 6 minutes
6. Meanwhile, melt the butter and combine with the honey and the rest of the seasoning
7. Remove the wings from the air fryer and pour the sauce over the top

Grain-free Chicken Katsu

Servings: 4

Cooking Time:xx

Ingredients:

- 125 g/1¼ cups ground almonds
- ½ teaspoon salt
- ½ teaspoon garlic powder
- ½ teaspoon dried parsley
- ½ teaspoon freshly ground black pepper
- ¼ teaspoon onion powder
- ¼ teaspoon dried oregano
- 450 g/1 lb. mini chicken fillets
- 1 egg, beaten
- oil, for spraying/drizzling
- coriander/cilantro leaves, to serve
- KATSU SAUCE
- 1 teaspoon olive oil or avocado oil
- 1 courgette/zucchini (approx. 150 g/5 oz.), finely chopped
- 1 carrot (approx. 100 g/3½ oz.), finely chopped
- 1 onion (approx. 120 g/4½ oz.), finely chopped
- 1 eating apple (approx. 150 g/5 oz.), cored and finely chopped
- 1 teaspoon ground ginger
- 1 teaspoon ground turmeric
- 2 teaspoons ground cumin
- 2 teaspoons ground coriander
- 1½ teaspoons mild chilli/chili powder
- 1 teaspoon garlic powder
- 1½ tablespoons runny honey
- 1 tablespoon soy sauce (gluten-free if you wish)
- 700 ml/3 cups vegetable stock (700 ml/3 cups water with 1½ stock cubes)

Directions:

1. First make the sauce. The easiest way to ensure all the vegetables and apple are finely chopped is to combine them in a food processor. Heat the oil in a large saucepan and sauté the finely chopped vegetables and apple for 5 minutes. Add all the seasonings, honey, soy sauce and stock and stir well, then bring to a simmer and simmer for 30 minutes.
2. Meanwhile, mix together the ground almonds, seasonings and spices. Dip each chicken fillet into the beaten egg, then into the almond-spice mix, making sure each fillet is fully coated. Spray the coated chicken fillets with olive oil (or simply drizzle over).
3. Preheat the air-fryer to 180ºC/350ºF.
4. Place the chicken fillets in the preheated air-fryer and air-fry for 10 minutes, turning halfway through cooking. Check the internal temperature of the chicken has reached at least 74ºC/165ºF using a meat thermometer – if not, cook for another few minutes.
5. Blend the cooked sauce in a food processor until smooth. Serve the chicken with the Katsu Sauce drizzled over (if necessary, reheat the sauce gently before serving) and scattered with coriander leaves. Any unused sauce can be frozen.

Garlic Parmesan Fried Chicken Wings

Servings: 4

Cooking Time:xx

Ingredients:

- 16 chicken wing drumettes
- Cooking spray
- 240ml low fat buttermilk
- 150g flour
- 140g grated parmesan
- 2 tbsp low sodium soy sauce
- 1 sachet of your favourite chicken seasoning
- 1 tsp garlic powder
- Salt and pepper to taste

Directions:

1. Place the chicken onto a cooking tray and pour the soy sauce over the top, ensuring it is fully coated
2. Season the chicken and place in the refrigerator for 30 minutes
3. Add the flour and parmesan into a ziplock bag
4. Coat the chicken with buttermilk and add it to the ziplock bag with the flour
5. Preheat your air fryer to 200ºC
6. Place the chicken into the air fryer for 20 minutes
7. Shake the air fryer basket every 5 minutes until the 20 minutes is up

Beef & Lamb And Pork Recipes

Sausage Gnocchi One Pot

Servings: 2
Cooking Time:xx

Ingredients:

- 4 links of sausage
- 250g green beans, washed and cut into halves
- 1 tsp Italian seasoning
- 1 tbsp olive oil
- 300g gnocchi
- Salt and pepper for seasoning

Directions:

1. Preheat the air fryer to 220ºC
2. Cut the sausage up into pieces
3. Take a bowl and add the gnocchi and green beans, along with the oil and season
4. Place the sausage into the fryer first and then the rest of the ingredients
5. Cook for 12 minutes, giving everything a stir halfway through

Vegetable & Beef Frittata

Servings: 2
Cooking Time:xx

Ingredients:

- 250g ground beef
- 4 shredded hash browns
- 8 eggs
- Half a diced onion
- 1 courgette, diced
- 250g grated cheese
- Salt and pepper for seasoning

Directions:

1. Break the ground beef up and place in the air fryer
2. Add the onion and combine well
3. Cook at 260ºC for 3 minutes
4. Stir the mixture and cook foremother 2 minutes
5. Remove and clean the tray
6. Add the courgette to the air fryer and spray with a little cooking oil
7. Cook for 3 minutes
8. Add to the meat mixture and combine
9. Take a mixing bowl and combine the cheese, has browns, and eggs
10. Add the meat and courgette to the bowl and season with salt and pepper
11. Take a 6" round baking tray and add the mixture
12. Cook for 8 minutes before cutting lines in the top and cooking for another 8 minutes
13. Cut into slices before serving

Parmesan Crusted Pork Chops

Servings: 6

Cooking Time:xx

Ingredients:

- 6 pork chops
- ½ tsp salt
- ¼ tsp pepper
- 1 tsp paprika
- 3 tbsp parmesan
- ½ tsp onion powder
- ¼ tsp chilli powder
- 2 eggs beaten
- 250g pork rind crumbs

Directions:

1. Preheat the air fryer to 200ºC
2. Season the pork with the seasonings
3. Place the pork rind into a food processor and blend into crumbs
4. Mix the pork rind and seasonings in a bowl
5. Beat the eggs in a separate bowl
6. Dip the pork into the egg then into the crumb mix
7. Place pork in the air fryer and cook for about 15 minutes until crispy

Lamb Burgers

Servings: 4

Cooking Time:xx

Ingredients:

- 600g minced lamb
- 2 tsp garlic puree
- 1 tsp harissa paste
- 2 tbsp Moroccan spice
- Salt and pepper

Directions:

1. Place all the ingredients in a bowl and mix well
2. Form into patties
3. Place in the air fryer and cook at 180ºC for 18 minutes

Fillet Mignon Wrapped In Bacon

Servings: 2

Cooking Time:xx

Ingredients:

- 1 kg filet mignon
- 500g bacon slices
- Olive oil

Directions:

1. Wrap the fillets in bacon
2. Season with salt and pepper and brush with olive oil
3. Place in the air fryer cook at 200ºC for 9 minutes turning halfway through

Pork Chops With Honey

Servings: 6
Cooking Time:xx
Ingredients:

- 2 ⅔ tbsp honey
- 100g ketchup
- 6 pork chops
- 2 cloves of garlic
- 2 slices mozzarella cheese

Directions:

1. Preheat air fryer to 200ºC
2. Mix all the ingredients together in a bowl
3. Add the pork chops, allow to marinate for at least 1 hour
4. Place in the air fryer and cook for about 12 minutes turning halfway

Carne Asada Chips

Servings: 2
Cooking Time:xx
Ingredients:

- 500g sirloin steak
- 1 bag of frozen French fries
- 350g grated cheese
- 2 tbsp sour cream
- 2 tbsp guacamole
- 2 tbsp steak seasoning
- Salt and pepper to taste

Directions:

1. Preheat your oven to 260ºC
2. Season the steak with the seasoning and a little salt and pepper
3. Place in the air fryer and cook for 4 minutes, before turning over and cooking for another 4 minutes
4. Remove and allow to rest
5. Add the French fries to the fryer and cook for 5 minutes, shaking regularly
6. Add the cheese
7. Cut the steak into pieces and add on top of the cheese
8. Cook for another 30 seconds, until the cheese is melted
9. Season

Cheesy Meatball Sub

Servings: 2
Cooking Time:xx
Ingredients:

- 8 frozen pork meatballs
- 5 tbsp marinara sauce
- 160g grated parmesan cheese
- 2 sub rolls or hotdog rolls
- 1/4 tsp dried oregano

Directions:

1. Preheat the air fryer to 220ºC
2. Place the meatball in the air fryer and cook for around 10 minutes, turning halfway through
3. Place the marinara sauce in a bowl
4. Add the meatballs to the sauce and coat completely
5. Add the oregano on top and coat once more
6. Take the bread roll and add the mixture inside
7. Top with the cheese
8. Place the meatball sub back in the air fryer and cook for 2 minutes until the bad is toasted and the cheese has melted

Beef Stroganoff

Servings:4

Cooking Time:20 Minutes

Ingredients:

- 4 cubes / 800 ml beef stock cubes
- 4 tbsp olive oil
- 1 onion, chopped
- 200 g / 7 oz sour cream
- 200 g / 7 oz mushroom, finely sliced
- 500 g / 17.6 oz steak, chopped
- 4 x 100 g / 3.5 oz egg noodles, cooked

Directions:

1. Preheat the air fryer to 200 °C / 400 °F and line the bottom of the basket with parchment paper.
2. Boil 800 ml of water and use it to dissolve the 4 beef stock cubes.
3. In a heat-proof bowl, mix the olive oil, onion, sour cream, mushrooms, and beef stock until fully combined.
4. Coat all sides of the steak chunks in the mixture and set aside to marinate for 10 minutes.
5. Transfer the steak to the air fryer, close the lid, and cook for 10 minutes. Serve the steak hot with a serving of egg noodles.

Steak And Mushrooms

Servings: 4

Cooking Time:xx

Ingredients:

- 500g cubed sirloin steak
- 300g button mushrooms
- 3 tbsp Worcestershire sauce
- 1 tbsp olive oil
- 1 tsp parsley flakes
- 1 tsp paprika
- 1 tsp crushed chilli flakes

Directions:

1. Combine all ingredients in a bowl, cover and chill for at least 4 hours
2. Preheat air fryer to 200ºC
3. Drain and discard the marinade from the steak
4. Place the steak and mushrooms in the air fryer and cook for 5 minutes
5. Toss and cook for a further 5 minutes

Honey & Mustard Meatballs

Servings: 4

Cooking Time:xx

Ingredients:

- 500g minced pork
- 1 red onion
- 1 tsp mustard
- 2 tsp honey
- 1 tsp garlic puree
- 1 tsp pork seasoning
- Salt and pepper

Directions:

1. Thinly slice the onion
2. Place all the ingredients in a bowl and mix until well combined
3. Form into meatballs, place in the air fryer and cook at 180ºC for 10 minutes

Bbq Ribs

Servings: 2
Cooking Time:xx
Ingredients:

- 500g ribs
- 3 chopped garlic cloves
- 4 tbsp bbq sauce
- 1 tbsp honey
- ½ tsp five spice
- 1 tsp sesame oil
- 1 tsp salt
- 1 tsp black pepper
- 1 tsp soy sauce

Directions:

1. Chop the ribs into small pieces and place them in a bowl
2. Add all the ingredients into the bowl and mix well
3. Marinate for 4 hours
4. Preheat the air fryer to 180ºC
5. Place the ribs into the air fryer and cook for 15 minutes
6. Coat the ribs in honey and cook for a further 15 minutes

Pork Belly With Crackling

Servings: 4
Cooking Time:xx
Ingredients:

- 800g belly pork
- 1 tsp sea salt
- 1 tsp garlic salt
- 2 tsp five spice
- 1 tsp rosemary
- 1 tsp white pepper
- 1 tsp sugar
- Half a lemon

Directions:

1. Cut lines into the meat portion of the belly pork
2. Cook thoroughly in water
3. Allow to air dry for 3 hours
4. Score the skin and prick holes with a fork
5. Rub with the dry rub mix, rub some lemon juice on the skin
6. Place in the air fryer and cook at 160ºC for 30 minutes then at 180ºC for a further 30 minutes

German Rouladen

Servings: 2
Cooking Time:xx

Ingredients:

- 2 tbsp oil
- 2 cups sliced onion
- 4 tbsp sour cream
- 1 tbsp tomato paste
- 1 tsp chopped parsley
- 400g steak
- ¼ cup dijon mustard
- 4 bacon strips

Directions:

1. Add salt and pepper to the onions and mix
2. Cook the onions in the air fryer at 200ºC for 5-6 minutes
3. Put half the onions in a bowl and mix with sour cream, 2 tsp parsley and tomato paste
4. Spread the mustard on to the steak then add the bacon and onion
5. Roll the steak up tightly and cook in the air fryer for 8-10 minutes

Pulled Pork, Bacon, And Cheese Sliders

Servings:2
Cooking Time:30 Minutes

Ingredients:

- 2 x 50 g / 3.5 oz pork steaks
- 1 tsp salt
- 1 tsp black pepper
- 4 slices bacon strips, chopped into small pieces
- 1 tbsp soy sauce
- 1 tbsp BBQ sauce
- 100 g / 7 oz cheddar cheese, grated
- 2 bread buns

Directions:

1. Preheat the air fryer to 200 °C / 400 °F and line the bottom of the basket with parchment paper.
2. Place the pork steaks on a clean surface and season with salt and black pepper. Move the pork steak in the prepared air fryer basket and cook for 15 minutes.
3. Remove the steak from the air fryer and shred using two forks. Mix with the chopped bacon in a heatproof bowl and place the bowl in the air fryer. Cook for 10 minutes.
4. Remove the bowl from the air fryer and stir in the soy sauce and BBQ sauce. Return the bowl to the air fryer basket and continue cooking for a further 5 minutes.
5. Meanwhile, spread the cheese across one half of the bread buns. Top with the cooked pulled pork and an extra squirt of BBQ sauce.

Beef Kebobs

Servings: 4
Cooking Time:xx

Ingredients:

- 500g cubed beef
- 25g low fat sour cream
- 2 tbsp soy sauce
- 8 x 6 inch skewers
- 1 bell pepper
- Half an onion

Directions:

1. Mix the sour cream and soy sauce in a bowl, add the cubed beef and marinate for at least 30 minutes
2. Cut the pepper and onion into 1 inch pieces, soak the skewers in water for 10 minutes
3. Thread beef, bell peppers and onion onto skewers
4. Cook in the air fryer at 200ºC for 10 minutes turning halfway

Cheese & Ham Sliders

Servings: 4
Cooking Time:xx

Ingredients:

- 8 slider bread rolls, cut in half
- 16 slices of sweet ham
- 16 slices of Swiss cheese
- 5 tbsp mayonnaise
- 1/2 tsp paprika
- 1 tsp onion powder
- 1 tsp dill

Directions:

1. Place 2 slices of ham into each bread roll and 2 slices of cheese
2. Take a bowl and combine the mayonnaise with the onion powder, dill and paprika
3. Add half a tablespoon of the sauce on top of each piece of cheese
4. Place the top on the bread slider
5. Cook at 220ºC for 5 minutes

Crispy Chili Sausages

Servings:4
Cooking Time:20 Minutes

Ingredients:

- 8 sausages, uncooked
- 2 eggs
- ½ tsp salt
- ½ black pepper
- ½ tsp chili flakes
- ½ tsp paprika

Directions:

1. Preheat the air fryer to 180 °C / 350 °F and line the bottom of the basket with parchment paper.
2. Place the sausages in the air fryer and cook for 5 minutes until slightly browned, but not fully cooked. Remove from the air fryer and set aside.
3. While the sausages are cooking, whisk together the eggs, salt, black pepper, chili flakes, and paprika. Coat the sausages evenly in the egg and spice mixture.
4. Return the sausages to the air fryer and cook for a further 5 minutes until brown and crispy.
5. Eat the sausages while hot with a side of steamed vegetables or place them in a sandwich for lunch.

Hamburgers

Servings: 4
Cooking Time:xx

Ingredients:

- 500g minced beef
- 1 grated onion
- Salt and pepper to taste

Directions:

1. Preheat air fryer to 200ºC
2. Place the grated onion and the beef into a bowl and combine together well
3. Divide minced beef into 4 equal portions, form into patties
4. Season with salt and pepper
5. Place in the air fryer and cook for 10 minutes, turnover and cook for a further 3 minutes

Tender Ham Steaks

Servings: 1

Cooking Time:xx

Ingredients:

- 1 ham steak
- 2 tbsp brown sugar
- 1 tsp honey
- 2 tbsp melted butter

Directions:

1. Preheat the air fryer to 220ºC
2. Combine the melted butter and brown sugar until smooth
3. Add the ham to the air fryer and brush both sides with the butter mixture
4. Cook for 12 minutes, turning halfway through and re-brushing the ham
5. Drizzle honey on top before serving

Beef Wellington

Servings: 4

Cooking Time:xx

Ingredients:

- 300g chicken liver pate
- 500g shortcrust pastry
- 600g beef fillet
- 1 egg beaten
- Salt and pepper

Directions:

1. Remove all the visible fat from the beef season with salt and pepper. Wrap in cling film and place in the fridge for 1 hour
2. Roll out the pastry, brush the edges with egg
3. Spread the pate over the pastry. Remove the clingfilm from the beef and place in the center of the pastry
4. Seal the pastry around the meat
5. Place in the air fryer and cook at 160ºC for 35 minutes

Japanese Pork Chops

Servings: 4

Cooking Time:xx

Ingredients:

- 6 boneless pork chops
- 30g flour
- 2 beaten eggs
- 2 tbsp sweet chilli sauce
- 500g cup seasoned breadcrumbs
- ⅛ tsp salt
- ⅛ tsp pepper
- Tonkatsu sauce to taste

Directions:

1. Place the flour, breadcrumbs and eggs in 3 separate bowls
2. Sprinkle both sides of the pork with salt and pepper
3. Coat the pork in flour, egg and then breadcrumbs
4. Place in the air fryer and cook at 180ºC for 8 minutes, turn then cook for a further 5 minutes
5. Serve with sauces on the side

Fish & Seafood Recipes

Sea Bass With Asparagus Spears

Servings: 2
Cooking Time:xx

Ingredients:

- 2 x 100-g/3½-oz. sea bass fillets
- 8 asparagus spears
- 2 teaspoons olive oil
- salt and freshly ground black pepper
- boiled new potatoes, to serve
- CAPER DRESSING
- 1½ tablespoons olive oil
- grated zest and freshly squeezed juice of ½ lemon
- 1 tablespoon small, jarred capers
- 1 teaspoon Dijon mustard
- 1 tablespoon freshly chopped flat-leaf parsley

Directions:

1. Preheat the air-fryer to 180ºC/350ºF.
2. Prepare the fish and asparagus by brushing both with the olive oil and sprinkling over salt and pepper.
3. Add the asparagus to the preheated air-fryer and air-fry for 4 minutes, then turn the asparagus and add the fish to the air-fryer drawer. Cook for a further 4 minutes. Check the internal temperature of the fish has reached at least 60ºC/140ºF using a meat thermometer – if not, cook for another minute.
4. Meanwhile, make the dressing by combining all the ingredients in a jar and shaking well. Pour the dressing over the cooked fish and asparagus spears and serve with new potatoes.

Extra Crispy Popcorn Shrimp

Servings: 2
Cooking Time:xx

Ingredients:

- 300g Frozen popcorn shrimp
- 1 tsp cayenne pepper
- Salt and pepper for seasoning

Directions:

1. Preheat the air fryer to 220ºC
2. Place the shrimp inside the air fryer and cook for 6 minutes, giving them a shake at the halfway point
3. Remove and season with salt and pepper, and the cayenne to your liking

Crispy Cajun Fish Fingers

Servings: 2
Cooking Time:xx
Ingredients:

- 350 g/12 oz. cod loins
- 1 teaspoon smoked paprika
- ½ teaspoon cayenne pepper
- ½ teaspoon onion granules
- ¾ teaspoon dried oregano
- ¼ teaspoon dried thyme
- ½ teaspoon salt
- ½ teaspoon unrefined sugar
- 40 g/½ cup dried breadcrumbs (gluten-free if you wish, see page 9)
- 2 tablespoons plain/all-purpose flour (gluten-free if you wish)
- 1 egg, beaten

Directions:

1. Slice the cod into 6 equal fish 'fingers'. Mix the spices, herbs, salt and sugar together, then combine with the breadcrumbs. Lay out three bowls: one with flour, one with beaten egg and one with the Cajun-spiced breadcrumbs. Dip each fish finger into the flour, then the egg, then the breadcrumbs until fully coated.
2. Preheat the air-fryer to 180ºC/350ºF.
3. Add the fish to the preheated air-fryer and air-fry for 6 minutes, until cooked inside. Check the internal temperature of the fish has reached at least 75ºC/167ºF using a meat thermometer – if not, cook for another few minutes.

Tandoori Salmon

Servings: 4
Cooking Time:xx
Ingredients:

- 300g salmon
- 1 tbsp butter
- 1 tbsp tandoori spice
- Salt and pepper to taste
- 1 small tomato
- Half a red onion
- 600g plain yogurt
- 30 fresh mint leaves, chopped
- 1 tsp minced green chilli
- 1 tbsp ground cumin
- Half a cucumber, chopped

Directions:

1. Cut the salmon into cubes and coat in the tandoori spice mix. Chill for 30 minutes to marinate
2. Blend mint, cumin and chilli with ¼ of the yogurt refrigerate and leave to steep
3. Peel the tomato and cut into cubes. Peel the cucumber and chop into cubes, finely dice the onion
4. Cook the salmon in the air fryer for 5-6 minutes at 200ºC
5. Mix the flavoured yogurt with the remaining yogurt, tomato, cucumber and onion
6. Place the sauce in serving bowls and place the salmon on top

Air Fryer Tuna

Servings: 2
Cooking Time:xx

Ingredients:

- 2 tuna steaks, boneless and skinless
- 2 tsp honey
- 1 tsp grated ginger
- 4 tbsp soy sauce
- 1 tsp sesame oil
- 1/2 tsp rice vinegar

Directions:

1. Combine the honey, soy sauce, rice vinegar and sesame oil in a bowl until totally mixed together
2. Cover the tuna steaks with the sauce and place in the refrigerator for half an hour to marinade
3. Preheat the air fryer to 270ºC
4. Cook the tuna for 4 minutes
5. Allow to rest before slicing

Oat & Parmesan Crusted Fish Fillets

Servings: 2
Cooking Time:xx

Ingredients:

- 20 g/⅓ cup fresh breadcrumbs
- 25 g/3 tablespoons oats
- 15 g/¼ cup grated Parmesan
- 1 egg
- 2 x 175-g/6-oz. white fish fillets, skin-on
- salt and freshly ground black pepper

Directions:

1. Preheat the air-fryer to 180ºC/350ºF.
2. Combine the breadcrumbs, oats and cheese in a bowl and stir in a pinch of salt and pepper. In another bowl beat the egg. Dip the fish fillets in the egg, then top with the oat mixture.
3. Add the fish fillets to the preheated air-fryer on an air-fryer liner or a piece of pierced parchment paper. Air-fry for 10 minutes. Check the fish is just flaking away when a fork is inserted, then serve immediately.

Honey Sriracha Salmon

Servings: 2
Cooking Time:xx

Ingredients:

- 25g sriracha
- 25g honey
- 500g salmon fillets
- 1 tbsp soy sauce

Directions:

1. Mix the honey, soy sauce and sriracha, keep half the mix to one side for dipping
2. Place the salmon in the sauce skin side up and marinade for 30 minutes
3. Spray air fryer basket with cooking spray
4. Heat the air fryer to 200ºC
5. Place salmon in the air fryer skin side down and cook for 12 minutes

Air Fryer Mussels

Servings: 2
Cooking Time:xx

Ingredients:

- 400g mussels
- 1 tbsp butter
- 200ml water
- 1 tsp basil
- 2 tsp minced garlic
- 1 tsp chives
- 1 tsp parsley

Directions:

1. Preheat air fryer to 200ºC
2. Clean the mussels, soak for 30 minutes, and remove the beard
3. Add all ingredients to an air fryer-safe pan
4. Cook for 3 minutes
5. Check to see if the mussels have opened, if not cook for a further 2 minutes. Once all mussels are open, they are ready to eat.

Mushrooms Stuffed With Crab

Servings: 2
Cooking Time:xx

Ingredients:

- 500g large mushrooms
- 2 tsp salt
- Half a diced red onion
- 2 diced celery sticks
- 300g lump crab
- 35g seasoned breadcrumbs
- 1 egg
- 1 tsp oregano
- 1 tsp hot sauce
- 50g grated Parmesan cheese

Directions:

1. Preheat to 260ºC
2. Take a baking sheet and arrange the mushrooms top down
3. Spray with a little cooking oil
4. Take a bowl and combine the onions, celery, breadcrumbs, egg, crab and half the cheese, oregano and hot sauce
5. Fill each mushroom with the mixture and make sure it's heaped over the top
6. Cover with the rest of the cheese
7. Place in the air fryer for 18 minutes

Fish In Parchment Paper

Servings: 2
Cooking Time:xx

Ingredients:

- 250g cod fillets
- 1 chopped carrot
- 1 chopped fennel
- 1 tbsp oil
- 1 thinly sliced red pepper
- ½ tsp tarragon
- 1 tbsp lemon juice
- 1 tbsp salt
- ½ tsp ground pepper

Directions:

1. In a bowl, mix the tarragon and ½ tsp salt add the vegetables and mix well
2. Cut two large squares of parchment paper
3. Spray the cod with oil and cover both sides with salt and pepper
4. Place the cod in the parchment paper and add the vegetables
5. Fold over the paper to hold the fish and vegetables
6. Place in the air fryer and cook at 170ºC for 15 minutes

Cajun Prawn Skewers

Servings: 2
Cooking Time:xx

Ingredients:

- 350 g/12 oz. king prawns/jumbo shrimp
- MARINADE
- 1 teaspoon smoked paprika
- 1 teaspoon unrefined sugar
- 1 teaspoon salt
- ½ teaspoon onion powder
- ½ teaspoon mustard powder
- ¼ teaspoon dried oregano
- ¼ teaspoon dried thyme
- 1 teaspoon white wine vinegar
- 2 teaspoons olive oil

Directions:

1. Mix all the marinade ingredients together in a bowl. Mix the prawns/shrimp into the marinade and cover. Place in the fridge to marinate for at least an hour.
2. Preheat the air-fryer to 180ºC/350ºF.
3. Thread 4–5 prawns/shrimp on to each skewer (you should have enough for 4–5 skewers). Add the skewers to the preheated air-fryer and air-fry for 2 minutes, then turn the skewers and cook for a further 2 minutes. Check the internal temperature of the prawns/shrimp has reached at least 50ºC/125ºF using a meat thermometer – if not, cook for another few minutes. Serve immediately.

Beer Battered Fish Tacos

Servings: 2
Cooking Time:xx

Ingredients:

- 300g cod fillets
- 2 eggs
- 1 can of Mexican beer
- 300g cornstarch
- 300g flour
- 2 soft corn tortillas
- ½ tsp chilli powder
- 1 tbsp cumin
- Salt and pepper to taste

Directions:

1. Whisk together the eggs and beer
2. In a separate bowl whisk together cornstarch, chilli powder, flour, cumin and salt and pepper
3. Coat the fish in the egg mixture then coat in flour mixture
4. Spray the air fryer with non stick spray and add the fish
5. Set your fryer to 170ºC and cook for 15 minutes
6. Place the fish in a corn tortilla

Gluten Free Honey And Garlic Shrimp

Servings: 2
Cooking Time:xx

Ingredients:

- 500g fresh shrimp
- 5 tbsp honey
- 2 tbsp gluten free soy sauce
- 2 tbsp tomato ketchup
- 250g frozen stir fry vegetables
- 1 crushed garlic clove
- 1 tsp fresh ginger
- 2 tbsp cornstarch

Directions:

1. Simmer the honey, soy sauce, garlic, tomato ketchup and ginger in a saucepan
2. Add the cornstarch and whisk until sauce thickens
3. Coat the shrimp with the sauce
4. Line the air fryer with foil and add the shrimp and vegetables
5. Cook at 180ºC for 10 minutes

Fish In Foil

Servings: 2
Cooking Time:xx

Ingredients:

- 1 tablespoon avocado oil or olive oil, plus extra for greasing
- 1 tablespoon soy sauce (or tamari)
- 1½ teaspoons freshly grated garlic
- 1½ teaspoons freshly grated ginger
- 1 small red chilli/chile, finely chopped
- 2 skinless, boneless white fish fillets (about 350 g/12 oz. total weight)

Directions:

1. Mix the oil, soy sauce, garlic, ginger and chilli/chile together. Brush a little oil onto two pieces of foil, then lay the fish in the centre of the foil. Spoon the topping mixture over the fish. Wrap the foil around the fish to make a parcel, with a gap above the fish but shallow enough to fit in your air-fryer basket.
2. Preheat the air-fryer to 180ºC/350ºF.
3. Add the foil parcels to the preheated air-fryer and air-fry for 7–10 minutes, depending on the thickness of your fillets. The fish should just flake when a fork is inserted. Serve immediately.

Shrimp With Yum Yum Sauce

Servings: 4
Cooking Time:xx

Ingredients:

- 400g peeled jumbo shrimp
- 1 tbsp soy sauce
- 1 tbsp garlic paste
- 1 tbsp ginger paste
- 4 tbsp mayo
- 2 tbsp ketchup
- 1 tbsp sugar
- 1 tsp paprika
- 1 tsp garlic powder

Directions:

1. Mix soy sauce, garlic paste and ginger paste in a bowl. Add the shrimp, allow to marinate for 15 minutes
2. In another bowl mix ketchup, mayo, sugar, paprika and the garlic powder to make the yum yum sauce.
3. Set the air fryer to 200ºC, place shrimp in the basket and cook for 8-10 minutes

Store-cupboard Fishcakes

Servings: 3
Cooking Time:xx

Ingredients:

- 400 g/14 oz. cooked potato – either mashed potato or the insides of jacket potatoes (see page 124)
- 2 x 150–200-g/5½–7-oz. cans fish, such as tuna or salmon, drained
- 2 eggs
- ¾ teaspoon salt
- 1 teaspoon dried parsley
- ½ teaspoon freshly ground black pepper
- 1 tablespoon olive oil
- caper dressing (see page 79), to serve

Directions:

1. Mix the cooked potato, fish, eggs, salt, parsley and pepper together in a bowl, then divide into 6 equal portions and form into fishcakes. Drizzle the olive oil over both sides of each fishcake.
2. Preheat the air-fryer to 180ºC/350ºF.
3. Add the fishcakes to the preheated air-fryer and air-fry for 15 minutes, turning halfway through cooking. Serve with salad and tartare sauce or Caper Dressing.

Maine Seafood

Servings: 2
Cooking Time:xx

Ingredients:

- 500g flour
- 400g breadcrumbs
- 300g steamer clams
- 3 eggs
- 3 tbsp water

Directions:

1. Soak the clams for 3 hours, drain and rinse
2. Bring 1 inch of water to boil, add the clams and cover with a lid, steam for about 7 minutes until the clams open.
3. Remove the clams from the shell and set aside
4. Put the eggs in a bowl and mix with the water
5. Dip the clams in the flour, then the egg and then coat in breadcrumbs
6. Heat the air fryer to 180ºC and cook for about 7 minutes

Copycat Fish Fingers

Servings: 2
Cooking Time:xx

Ingredients:

- 2 slices wholemeal bread, grated into breadcrumbs
- 50g plain flour
- 1 beaten egg
- 1 white fish fillet
- The juice of 1 small lemon
- 1 tsp parsley
- 1 tsp thyme
- 1 tsp mixed herbs
- Salt and pepper to taste

Directions:

1. Preheat the air fryer to 180ºC
2. Add salt pepper and parsley to the breadcrumbs and combine well
3. Place the egg in another bowl
4. Place the flour in a separate bowl
5. Place the fish into a food processor and add the lemon juice, salt, pepper thyme and mixed herbs
6. Blitz to create a crumb-like consistency
7. Roll your fish in the flour, then the egg and then the breadcrumbs
8. Cook at 180ºC for 8 minutes

Garlic-parsley Prawns

Servings: 2
Cooking Time:xx

Ingredients:

- 300 g/10½ oz. raw king prawns/jumbo shrimp (without shell)
- 40 g/3 tablespoons garlic butter, softened (see page 72)
- 2 tablespoons freshly chopped flat-leaf parsley

Directions:

1. Thread the prawns/shrimp onto 6 metal skewers that will fit your air-fryer. Mix together the softened garlic butter and parsley and brush evenly onto the prawn skewers.
2. Preheat the air-fryer to 180ºC/350ºF.
3. Place the skewers on an air-fryer liner or a piece of pierced parchment paper. Add the skewers to the preheated air-fryer and air-fry for 2 minutes, then turn the skewers over and cook for a further 2 minutes. Check the internal temperature of the prawns has reached at least 50ºC/120ºF using a meat thermometer – if not, cook for another few minutes and serve.

Air Fried Scallops

Servings: 2
Cooking Time:xx

Ingredients:

- 6 scallops
- 1 tbsp olive oil
- Salt and pepper to taste

Directions:

1. Brush the filets with olive oil
2. Sprinkle with salt and pepper
3. Place in the air fryer and cook at 200ºC for 2 mins
4. Turn the scallops over and cook for another 2 minutes

Pesto Salmon

Servings: 4
Cooking Time:xx

Ingredients:

- 4 x 150–175-g/5½–6-oz. salmon fillets
- lemon wedges, to serve
- PESTO
- 50 g/scant ½ cup toasted pine nuts
- 50 g/2 oz. fresh basil
- 50 g/⅔ cup grated Parmesan or Pecorino
- 100 ml/7 tablespoons olive oil

Directions:

1. To make the pesto, blitz the pine nuts, basil and Parmesan to a paste in a food processor. Pour in the olive oil and process again.
2. Preheat the air-fryer to 160ºC/325ºF.
3. Top each salmon fillet with 2 tablespoons of the pesto. Add the salmon fillets to the preheated air-fryer and air-fry for 9 minutes. Check the internal temperature of the fish has reached at least 63ºC/145ºF using a meat thermometer – if not, cook for another few minutes.

Garlic Tilapia

Servings: 2
Cooking Time:xx

Ingredients:

- 2 tilapia fillets
- 2 tsp chopped fresh chives
- 2 tsp chopped fresh parsley
- 2 tsp olive oil
- 1 tsp minced garlic
- Salt and pepper for seasoning

Directions:

1. Preheat the air fryer to 220ºC
2. Take a small bowl and combine the olive oil with the chives, garlic, parsley and a little salt and pepper
3. Brush the mixture over the fish fillets
4. Place the fish into the air fryer and cook for 10 minutes, until flaky

Vegetarian & Vegan Recipes

Arancini

Servings: 12

Cooking Time:xx

Ingredients:

- 1 batch of risotto
- 100g panko breadcrumbs
- 1 tsp onion powder
- Salt and pepper
- 300ml warm marinara sauce

Directions:

1. Take ¼ cup risotto and form a rice ball
2. Mix the panko crumbs, onion powder, salt and pepper
3. Coat the risotto ball in the crumb mix
4. Place in the air fryer, spray with oil and cook at 200ºC for 10 minutes
5. Serve with marinara sauce

Chickpea Falafel

Servings: 2

Cooking Time:xx

Ingredients:

- 400-g/14-oz can chickpeas, drained and rinsed
- 3 tablespoons freshly chopped coriander/cilantro
- 1 plump garlic clove, chopped
- freshly squeezed juice of ½ a lemon
- 1 teaspoon ground cumin
- 1 teaspoon smoked paprika
- 1 teaspoon salt
- 2 teaspoons olive oil (plus extra in a spray bottle or simply drizzle over)
- ½ teaspoon chilli/hot red pepper flakes

Directions:

1. In a food processor combine all the ingredients except the chilli/hot red pepper flakes. Divide the mixture into 6 equal portions and mould into patties.
2. Preheat the air-fryer to 180ºC/350ºF.
3. Spray each falafel with extra olive oil and sprinkle with chilli/hot red pepper flakes, then place in the preheated air-fryer and air-fry for 7 minutes, or until just brown on top. Remove carefully and serve.

Courgette Burgers

Servings: 4
Cooking Time:xx

Ingredients:

- 1 courgette
- 1 small can of chickpeas, drained
- 3 spring onions
- Pinch of dried garlic
- Salt and pepper
- 3 tbsp coriander
- 1 tsp chilli powder
- 1 tsp mixed spice
- 1 tsp cumin

Directions:

1. Grate the courgette and drain the excess water
2. Thinly slice the spring onions and add to the bowl with the chickpeas, courgette and seasoning
3. Bind the ingredients and form into patties
4. Place in the air fryer and cook for 12 minutes at 200ºC

Baked Aubergine Slices With Yogurt Dressing

Servings: 2
Cooking Time:xx

Ingredients:

- 1 aubergine/eggplant, sliced 1.5 cm/⅝ in. thick
- 3 tablespoons olive oil
- ½ teaspoon salt
- YOGURT DRESSING
- 1 small garlic clove
- 1 tablespoon tahini or nut butter
- 100 g/½ cup Greek yogurt
- 2 teaspoons freshly squeezed lemon juice
- 1 tablespoon runny honey
- a pinch of salt
- a pinch of ground cumin
- a pinch of sumac
- TO SERVE
- 30 g/1 oz. rocket/arugula
- 2 tablespoons freshly chopped mint
- 3 tablespoons pomegranate seeds

Directions:

1. Preheat the air-fryer to 180ºC/350ºF.
2. Drizzle the olive oil over each side of the aubergine/eggplant slices. Sprinkle with salt. Add the aubergines to the preheated air-fryer and air-fry for 10 minutes, turning halfway through cooking.
3. Meanwhile, make the dressing by combining all the ingredients in a mini food processor (alterantively, finely chop the garlic, add to a jar with the other ingredients and shake vigorously).
4. Serve the cooked aubergine slices on a bed of rocket/arugula, drizzled with the dressing and with the mint and pomegranate seeds scattered over the top.

Shakshuka

Servings: 2
Cooking Time:xx

Ingredients:

- 2 eggs
- BASE
- 100 g/3½ oz. thinly sliced (bell) peppers
- 1 red onion, halved and thinly sliced
- 2 medium tomatoes, chopped
- 2 teaspoons olive oil
- ¼ teaspoon salt
- ¼ teaspoon freshly ground black pepper
- ½ teaspoon chilli/hot red pepper flakes
- SAUCE
- 100 g/3½ oz. passata/strained tomatoes
- 1 tablespoon tomato purée/paste
- 1 teaspoon balsamic vinegar
- ½ teaspoon runny honey
- ½ teaspoon ground cumin
- ½ teaspoon paprika
- ¼ teaspoon salt
- ⅛ teaspoon freshly ground black pepper

Directions:

1. Preheat the air-fryer to 180ºC/350ºF.
2. Combine the base ingredients together in a baking dish that fits inside your air-fryer. Add the dish to the preheated air-fryer and air-fry for 10 minutes, stirring halfway through cooking.
3. Meanwhile, combine the sauce ingredients in a bowl. Pour this into the baking dish when the 10 minutes are up. Stir, then make a couple of wells in the sauce for the eggs. Crack the eggs into the wells, then cook for a further 5 minutes or until the eggs are just cooked and yolks still runny. Remove from the air-fryer and serve.

Whole Wheat Pizza

Servings: 2
Cooking Time:xx

Ingredients:

- 100g marinara sauce
- 2 whole wheat pitta
- 200g baby spinach leaves
- 1 small plum tomato, sliced
- 1 clove garlic, sliced
- 400g grated cheese
- 50g shaved parmesan

Directions:

1. Preheat air fryer to 160ºC
2. Spread each of the pitta with marinara sauce
3. Sprinkle with cheese, top with spinach, plum tomato and garlic. Finish with parmesan shavings
4. Place in the air fryer and cook for about 4 mins cheese has melted

Ravioli Air Fryer Style

Servings: 4
Cooking Time:xx

Ingredients:

- Half a pack of frozen ravioli
- 200g Italian breadcrumbs
- 200ml buttermilk
- 5 tbsp marinara sauce
- 1 tbsp olive oil

Directions:

1. Preheat the air fryer to 220ºC
2. Place the buttermilk in a bowl
3. Add the breadcrumbs to another bowl
4. Take each piece of ravioli and dip it first into the buttermilk and then into the breadcrumbs, coating evenly
5. Add the ravioli to the air fryer and cook for 7 minutes, adding a small amount of oil at the halfway point
6. Serve with the marinara sauce on the side

Air-fried Artichoke Hearts

Servings: 7
Cooking Time:xx

Ingredients:

- 14 artichoke hearts
- 200g flour
- ¼ tsp baking powder
- Salt
- 6 tbsp water
- 6 tbsp breadcrumbs
- ¼ tsp basil
- ¼ tsp oregano
- ¼ tsp garlic powder
- ¼ tsp paprika

Directions:

1. Mix the baking powder, salt, flour and water in a bowl
2. In another bowl combine the breadcrumbs and seasonings
3. Dip the artichoke in the batter then coat in breadcrumbs
4. Place in the air fryer and cook at 180ºC for 8 minutes

Vegan Meatballs

Servings:4
Cooking Time:15 Minutes

Ingredients:

- 2 tbsp olive oil
- 2 tbsp soy sauce
- 1 onion, finely sliced
- 1 large carrot, peeled and grated
- 1 x 400 g / 14 oz can chickpeas, drained and rinsed
- 50 g / 1.8 oz plain flour
- 50 g / 1.8 oz rolled oats
- 2 tbsp roasted cashews, chopped
- 1 tsp garlic powder
- ½ tsp cumin

Directions:

1. Preheat the air fryer to 175 °C / 350 °F and line the air fryer with parchment paper or grease it with olive oil.
2. In a large mixing bowl, combine the olive oil and soy sauce. Add the onion slices and grated carrot and toss to coat in the sauce.
3. Place the vegetables in the air fryer and cook for 5 minutes until slightly soft.
4. Meanwhile, place the chickpeas, plain flour, rolled oats, and roasted cashews in a blender, and mix until well combined.
5. Remove the mixture from the blender and stir in the garlic powder and cumin. Add the onions and carrots to the bowl and mix well.
6. Scoop the mixture into small meatballs and place them into the air fryer. Increase the temperature on the machine up to 190 °C / 370 °F and cook the meatballs for 10-12 minutes until golden and crispy.

Cheese, Tomato & Pesto Crustless Quiches

Servings: 1–2
Cooking Time:xx

Ingredients:

- 40 g/½ cup grated mature Cheddar
- 3 eggs, beaten
- 3 cherry tomatoes, finely chopped
- salt and freshly ground black pepper
- ½ teaspoon olive oil, to grease ramekins
- 2 tablespoons pesto (jarred or see page 80)

Directions:

1. Preheat the air-fryer to 180ºC/350ºF.
2. Mix together the cheese, eggs, tomatoes, salt and pepper in a bowl.
3. Grease the ramekins with the oil (and line with parchment paper if you wish to remove the quiches to serve). Pour the egg mixture into the ramekins.
4. Place the ramekins in the preheated air-fryer and air-fry for 10 minutes, stirring the contents of the ramekins halfway through cooking. Serve hot with 1 tablespoon pesto drizzled over each quiche.

Stuffed Peppers

Servings: 6
Cooking Time:xx

Ingredients:

- 250g diced potatoes
- 100g peas
- 1 small onion, diced
- 1 carrot, diced
- 1 bread roll, diced
- 2 garlic cloves, minced
- 2 tsp mixed herbs
- 6 bell peppers
- 100g grated cheese

Directions:

1. Preheat air fryer to 180ºC
2. Combine all the ingredients together apart from the peppers
3. Stuff the peppers with the mix
4. Place in the air fryer and cook for about 20 minutes

Bbq Sandwich

Servings: 2
Cooking Time:xx

Ingredients:

- 1 tbsp mayo
- ¼ tsp white wine vinegar
- ¼ tsp lemon juice
- 1/8 tsp garlic powder
- Pinch of salt
- Cabbage mix
- 2 sandwich buns
- 150g bbq soy curls

Directions:

1. Mix mayo, white wine vinegar, lemon juice, cabbage mix, garlic powder and pinch of salt to make coleslaw. Set aside
2. Add the buns to the air fryer and cook at 200ºC for 5 minutes to toast
3. Fill the buns with coleslaw, soy curls, pickles and chopped onions

Two-step Pizza

Servings: 1
Cooking Time:xx
Ingredients:

- BASE
- 130 g/generous ½ cup Greek yogurt
- 125 g self-raising/self-rising flour, plus extra for dusting
- ¼ teaspoon salt
- PIZZA SAUCE
- 100 g/3½ oz. passata/strained tomatoes
- 1 teaspoon dried oregano
- ¼ teaspoon garlic salt
- TOPPINGS
- 75 g/2½ oz. mozzarella, torn
- fresh basil leaves, to garnish

Directions:

1. Mix together the base ingredients in a bowl. Once the mixture starts to look crumbly, use your hands to bring the dough together into a ball. Transfer to a piece of floured parchment paper and roll to about 5 mm/¼ in. thick. Transfer to a second piece of non-floured parchment paper.
2. Preheat the air-fryer to 200ºC/400ºF.
3. Meanwhile, mix the pizza sauce ingredients together in a small bowl and set aside.
4. Prick the pizza base all over with a fork and transfer (on the parchment paper) to the preheated air-fryer and air-fry for 5 minutes. Turn the pizza base over and top with the pizza sauce and the torn mozzarella. Cook for a further 3–4 minutes, until the cheese has melted. Serve immediately with the basil scattered over the top.

Jackfruit Taquitos

Servings: 2
Cooking Time:xx
Ingredients:

- 1 large Jackfruit
- 250g red beans
- 100g pico de gallo sauce
- 50ml water
- 2 tbsp water
- 4 wheat tortillas
- Olive oil spray

Directions:

1. Place the jackfruit, red beans, sauce and water in a saucepan
2. Bring to the boil and simmer for 25 minutes
3. Preheat the air fryer to 185ºC
4. Mash the jackfruit mixture, add ¼ cup of the mix to each tortilla and roll up tightly
5. Spray with olive oil and place in the air fryer
6. Cook for 8 minutes

Buffalo Cauliflower Bites

Servings: 4
Cooking Time:xx
Ingredients:

- 3 tbsp ketchup
- 2 tbsp hot sauce
- 1 large egg white
- 200g panko bread crumbs
- 400g cauliflower
- ¼ tsp black pepper
- Cooking spray
- 40g sour cream
- 40g blue cheese
- 1 garlic clove, grated
- 1 tsp red wine vinegar

Directions:

1. Whisk together ketchup, hot sauce and egg white
2. Place the breadcrumbs in another bowl
3. Dip the cauliflower in the sauce then in the breadcrumbs
4. Coat with cooking spray
5. Place in the air fryer and cook at 160ºC for about 20 minutes until crispy
6. Mix remaining ingredients together and serve as a dip

Roast Cauliflower & Broccoli

Servings: 6
Cooking Time:xx
Ingredients:

- 300g broccoli
- 300g cauliflower
- 2 tbsp oil
- ½ tsp garlic powder
- ¼ tsp salt
- ¼ tsp paprika
- ⅛ tsp pepper

Directions:

1. Preheat air fryer to 200ºC
2. Place broccoli and cauliflower in a bowl and microwave for 3 minutes
3. Add remaining ingredients and mix well
4. Add to the air fryer and cook for about 12 mins

Vegan Fried Ravioli

Servings: 4
Cooking Time:xx

Ingredients:

- 100g panko breadcrumbs
- 2 tsp yeast
- 1 tsp basil
- 1 tsp oregano
- 1 tsp garlic powder
- Pinch salt and pepper
- 50ml liquid from can of chickpeas
- 150g vegan ravioli
- Cooking spray
- 50g marinara for dipping

Directions:

1. Combine the breadcrumbs, yeast, basil, oregano, garlic powder and salt and pepper
2. Put the liquid from the chickpeas in a bowl
3. Dip the ravioli in the liquid then dip into the breadcrumb mix
4. Heat the air fryer to 190ºC
5. Place the ravioli in the air fryer and cook for about 6 minutes until crispy

Pakoras

Servings: 8
Cooking Time:xx

Ingredients:

- 200g chopped cauliflower
- 100g diced pepper
- 250g chickpea flour
- 30ml water
- ½ tsp cumin
- Cooking spray
- 1 onion, diced
- 1 tsp salt
- 1 garlic clove, minced
- 1 tsp curry powder
- 1 tsp coriander
- ½ tsp cayenne

Directions:

1. Preheat air fryer to 175ºC
2. Place all ingredients in a bowl and mix well
3. Spray cooking basket with oil
4. Spoon 2 tbsp of mix into the basket and flatten, continue until the basket is full
5. Cook for 8 minutes, turn then cook for a further 8 minutes

Mini Quiche

Servings: 2
Cooking Time:xx

Ingredients:

- 100g raw cashews
- 3 tbsp milk
- ½ tsp hot sauce
- 1 tsp white miso paste
- 1 tsp mustard
- 300g tofu
- 100g bacon pieces
- 1 chopped red pepper
- 1 chopped onion
- 6 tbsp yeast
- ½ tsp onion powder
- ½ tsp paprika
- ½ tsp cumin
- ½ tsp chilli powder
- ½ tsp black pepper
- ⅛ tsp turmeric
- ½ tsp canola oil
- 50g curly kale

Directions:

1. Heat the oil in a pan, add the bacon pepper, onion and curly kale and cook for about 3 minutes
2. Place all the other ingredients into a blender and blend until smooth
3. Add to a bowl with the bacon, pepper, onion and curly kale and mix well
4. Fill silicone muffin cups with the mix
5. Place in the air fryer and cook at 165ºC for 15 minutes

Quinoa-stuffed Romano Peppers

Servings: 2
Cooking Time:xx

Ingredients:

- 1 tablespoon olive oil
- 1 onion, diced
- 1 garlic clove, chopped
- 100 g/⅔ cup uncooked quinoa
- 1½ tablespoons fajita seasoning
- 140 g/1 cup canned sweetcorn/corn kernels (drained weight)
- 3 romano peppers, sliced lengthways, seeds removed but stalk left intact
- 60 g/⅔ cup grated mature Cheddar

Directions:

1. Heat the oil in a saucepan. Add the onion and garlic and sauté for 5 minutes, until soft. Add the quinoa, fajita seasoning and 250 ml/1 cup water. Bring to a simmer, then cover with a lid and simmer for 15 minutes or until the quinoa is cooked and the water absorbed. Stir in the sweetcorn/corn kernels. Stuff each pepper half with the quinoa mixture, then top with grated cheese.
2. Preheat the air-fryer to 180ºC/350ºF.
3. Place the peppers on an air-fryer liner or a piece of pierced parchment paper, place in the preheated air-fryer and air-fry for 12–14 minutes, depending how ‘chargrilled’ you like your peppers.

Air Fryer Cheese Sandwich

Servings:2
Cooking Time:10 Minutes

Ingredients:

- 4 slices white or wholemeal bread
- 2 tbsp butter
- 50 g / 3.5 oz cheddar cheese, grated

Directions:

1. Preheat the air fryer to 180 °C / 350 °F and line the bottom of the basket with parchment paper.
2. Lay the slices of bread out on a clean surface and butter one side of each. Evenly sprinkle the cheese on two of the slices and cover with the final two slices.
3. Transfer the sandwiches to the air fryer, close the lid, and cook for 5 minutes until the bread is crispy and golden, and the cheese is melted.

Falafel Burgers

Servings: 2
Cooking Time:xx

Ingredients:

- 1 large can of chickpeas
- 1 onion
- 1 lemon
- 140g oats
- 28g grated cheese
- 28g feta cheese
- Salt and pepper to taste
- 3 tbsp Greek yogurt
- 4 tbsp soft cheese
- 1 tbsp garlic puree
- 1 tbsp coriander
- 1 tbsp oregano
- 1 tbsp parsley

Directions:

1. Place the chickpeas, onion, lemon rind, garlic and seasonings and blend until coarse
2. Add the mix to a bowl and stir in half the soft cheese, cheese and feta
3. Form in to burger shape and coat in the oats
4. Place in the air fryer and cook at 180ºC for 8 minutes
5. To make the sauce mix the remaining soft cheese, greek yogurt and lemon juice in a bowl

Side Dishes Recipes

Alternative Stuffed Potatoes

Servings: 4
Cooking Time:xx
Ingredients:

- 4 baking potatoes, peeled and halved
- 1 tbsp olive oil
- 150g grated cheese
- ½ onion, diced
- 2 slices bacon

Directions:

1. Preheat air fryer to 175ºC
2. Brush the potatoes with oil and cook in the air fryer for 10 minutes
3. Coat again with oil and cook for a further 10 minutes
4. Cut the potatoes in half spoon the insides into a bowl and mix in the cheese
5. Place the bacon and onion in a pan and cook until browned, mix in with the potato
6. Stuff the skins with the mix and return to the air fryer, cook for about 6 minutes

Whole Sweet Potatoes

Servings: 4 As A Side Or Snack
Cooking Time:xx
Ingredients:

- 4 medium sweet potatoes
- 1 tablespoon olive oil
- 1 teaspoon salt
- toppings of your choice

Directions:

1. Preheat the air-fryer to 200ºC/400ºF.
2. Wash and remove any imperfections from the skin of the sweet potatoes, then rub the potatoes with the olive oil and salt.
3. Add the sweet potatoes to the preheated air-fryer and air-fry for up to 40 minutes (the cooking time depends on the size of the potatoes). Remove as soon as they are soft when pierced. Slice open and serve with your choice of toppings.
4. VARIATION: WHOLE JACKET POTATOES
5. Regular baking potatoes can be air-fried in the same way, but will require a cooking time of 45–60 minutes, depending on their size.

Bbq Beetroot Crisps

Servings:4
Cooking Time:5 Minutes
Ingredients:

- 400 g / 14 oz beetroot, sliced
- 2 tbsp olive oil
- 1 tbsp BBQ seasoning
- ½ tsp black pepper

Directions:

1. Preheat the air fryer to 180 °C / 350 °F and line the bottom of the basket with parchment paper.
2. Place the beetroot slices in a large bowl. Add the olive oil, BBQ seasoning, and black pepper, and toss to coat the beetroot slices on both sides.
3. Place the beetroot slices in the air fryer and cook for 5 minutes until hot and crispy.

Corn On The Cob

Servings: 4
Cooking Time:xx

Ingredients:

- 75g mayo
- 2 tsp grated cheese
- 1 tsp lime juice
- ¼ tsp chilli powder
- 2 ears of corn, cut into 4

Directions:

1. Heat the air fryer to 200ºC
2. Mix the mayo, cheese lime juice and chilli powder in a bowl
3. Cover the corn in the mayo mix
4. Place in the air fryer and cook for 8 minutes

Butternut Squash Fries

Servings: 4
Cooking Time:xx

Ingredients:

- 400g butternut squash, cut into sticks
- 1 tbsp olive oil
- 2 tbsp bagel seasoning
- 1 tsp fresh chopped rosemary

Directions:

1. Preheat air fryer to 200ºC
2. Drizzle butternut squash with olive oil mix to coat
3. Add to the air fryer, cook for about 22 minutes until golden brown, stirring every 4 minutes
4. Sprinkle with bagel seasoning to serve

Stuffing Filled Pumpkin

Servings: 2
Cooking Time:xx

Ingredients:

- 1/2 small pumpkin
- 1 diced parsnip
- 1 sweet potato, diced
- 1 diced onion
- 2 tsp dried mixed herbs
- 50g peas
- 1 carrot, diced
- 1 egg
- 2 minced garlic cloves

Directions:

1. Remove the seeds from the pumpkin
2. Combine all the other ingredients in a bowl
3. Stuff the pumpkin
4. Preheat the air fryer to 175ºC
5. Place the pumpkin in the air fryer and cook for about 30 minutes

Sweet Potato Tots

Servings: 24
Cooking Time:xx

Ingredients:

- 2 sweet potatoes, peeled
- ½ tsp cajun seasoning
- Olive oil cooking spray
- Sea salt to taste

Directions:

1. Boil the sweet potatoes in a pan for about 15 minutes, allow to cool
2. Grate the sweet potato and mix in the cajun seasoning
3. Form into tot shaped cylinders
4. Spray the air fryer with oil, place the tots in the air fryer
5. Sprinkle with salt and cook for 8 minutes at 200ºC, turn and cook for another 8 minutes

Celery Root Fries

Servings: 2
Cooking Time:xx

Ingredients:

- ½ celeriac, cut into sticks
- 500ml water
- 1 tbsp lime juice
- 1 tbsp olive oil
- 75g mayo
- 1 tbsp mustard
- 1 tbsp powdered horseradish

Directions:

1. Put celeriac in a bowl, add water and lime juice, soak for 30 minutes
2. Preheat air fryer to 200
3. Mix together the mayo, horseradish powder and mustard, refrigerate
4. Drain the celeriac, drizzle with oil and season with salt and pepper
5. Place in the air fryer and cook for about 10 minutes turning halfway
6. Serve with the mayo mix as a dip

Butternut Squash

Servings: 4
Cooking Time:xx

Ingredients:

- 500 g/1 lb. 2 oz. butternut squash, chopped into 2.5-cm/1-in. cubes
- 1 tablespoon olive oil or avocado oil
- 1 teaspoon smoked paprika
- 1 teaspoon dried oregano
- ½ teaspoon salt
- ¼ teaspoon freshly ground black pepper

Directions:

1. Preheat the air-fryer to 180ºC/350ºF.
2. In a bowl toss the butternut squash cubes in the oil and all the seasonings.
3. Add the butternut squash cubes to the preheated air-fryer and air-fry for 16–18 minutes, shaking the drawer once during cooking.

Roasted Okra

Servings: 1
Cooking Time:xx

Ingredients:

- 300g Okra, ends trimmed and pods sliced
- 1 tsp olive oil
- ¼ tsp salt
- ⅛ tsp pepper

Directions:

1. Preheat the air fryer to 175ºC
2. Combine all ingredients in a bowl and stir gently
3. Place in the air fryer and cook for 5 minutes, shake and cook for another 5 minutes

Hasselback New Potatoes

Servings: 4
Cooking Time:xx

Ingredients:

- 8–12 new potatoes, roughly 5–7 cm/2–2¾ in. in length
- 2 teaspoons olive oil
- salt
- 1 tablespoon butter (optional)

Directions:

1. Preheat the air-fryer to 180ºC/350ºF.
2. Slice the potatoes multiple times widthways, making sure you do not cut all the way through (if you place the potatoes in the bowl of a wooden spoon to make these slices, it prevents you cutting all the way through). Coat the potatoes in the olive oil and sprinkle over the salt.
3. Add the potatoes to the preheated air-fryer and air-fry for 20–25 minutes until the potatoes are crispy on the outside but soft on the inside. Serve immediately.

Honey Roasted Parsnips

Servings: 4
Cooking Time:xx

Ingredients:

- 350 g/12 oz. parsnips
- 1 tablespoon plain/all-purpose flour (gluten-free if you wish)
- 1½ tablespoons runny honey
- 2 tablespoons olive oil
- salt

Directions:

1. Top and tail the parsnips, then slice lengthways, about 2 cm/¾ in. wide. Place in a saucepan with water to cover and a good pinch of salt. Bring to the boil, then boil for 5 minutes.
2. Remove and drain well, allowing any excess water to evaporate. Dust the parsnips with flour. Mix together the honey and oil in a small bowl, then toss in the parsnips to coat well in the honey and oil.
3. Preheat the air-fryer to 180ºC/350ºF.
4. Add the parsnips to the preheated air-fryer and air-fry for 14–16 minutes, depending on how dark you like the outsides (the longer you cook them, the sweeter they get).

Courgette Gratin

Servings: 2
Cooking Time:xx

Ingredients:

- 2 courgette
- 1 tbsp chopped parsley
- 2 tbsp breadcrumbs
- 4 tbsp grated parmesan
- 1 tbsp vegetable oil
- Salt and pepper to taste

Directions:

1. Heat the air fryer to 180ºC
2. Cut each courgette in half length ways then slice
3. Mix the remaining ingredients together
4. Place the courgette in the air fryer and top with the breadcrumb mix
5. Cook for about 15 minutes until golden brown

Sweet And Sticky Parsnips And Carrots

Servings:2
Cooking Time:15 Minutes

Ingredients:

- 4 large carrots, peeled and chopped into long chunks
- 4 large parsnips, peeled and chopped into long chunks
- 1 tbsp olive oil
- 2 tbsp honey
- 1 tsp dried mixed herbs

Directions:

1. Preheat the air fryer to 150 °C / 300 °F and line the bottom of the basket with parchment paper.
2. Place the chopped carrots and parsnips in a large bowl and drizzle over the olive oil and honey. Sprinkle in some black pepper to taste and toss well to fully coat the vegetables.
3. Transfer the coated vegetables into the air fryer basket and shut the lid. Cook for 20 minutes until the carrots and parsnips and cooked and crispy.
4. Serve as a side with your dinner.

Orange Sesame Cauliflower

Servings: 4
Cooking Time:xx

Ingredients:

- 100ml water
- 30g cornstarch
- 50g flour
- 1/2 tsp salt
- ½ tsp pepper
- 2 tbsp tomato ketchup
- 2 tbsp brown sugar
- 1 sliced onion

Directions:

1. Mix together flour, cornstarch, water, salt and pepper until smooth
2. Coat the cauliflower and chill for 30 minutes
3. Place in the air fryer and cook for 22 minutes at 170ºC
4. Meanwhile combine remaining ingredients in a saucepan, gently simmer until thickened.
5. Mix cauliflower with sauce and top with toasted sesame seeds to serve

Ricotta Stuffed Aubergine

Servings: 2
Cooking Time:xx

Ingredients:

- 1 aubergine
- 150g ricotta cheese
- 75g Parmesan cheese, plus an extra 75g for the breading
- 1 tsp garlic powder
- 3 tbsp parsley
- 1 egg, plus an extra 2 eggs for the breading
- 300g pork rind crumbs
- 2 tsp Italian seasoning

Directions:

1. Cut the aubergine into rounds, about 1/2" in thickness
2. Line a baking sheet with parchment and arrange the rounds on top, sprinkling with salt
3. Place another sheet of parchment on top and place something heavy on top to get rid of excess water
4. Leave for 30 minutes
5. Take a bowl and combine the egg, ricotta, 75g Parmesan and parsley, until smooth
6. Remove the parchment from the aubergine and wipe off the salt
7. Take a tablespoon of the ricotta mixture and place on top of each round of aubergine, spreading with a knife
8. Place in the freezer for a while to set
9. Take a bowl and add the two eggs, the pork rinds, parmesan and seasonings, and combine
10. Remove the aubergine from the freezer and coat each one in the mixture completely
11. Place back in the freezer for 45 minutes
12. Cook in the air fryer for 8 minutes at 250ºC

Courgette Chips

Servings: 4
Cooking Time:xx

Ingredients:

- 250g panko bread crumbs
- 100g grated parmesan
- 1 medium courgette, thinly sliced
- 1 egg beaten

Directions:

1. Preheat the air fryer to 175ºC
2. Combine the breadcrumbs and parmesan
3. Dip the courgette into the egg then coat in bread crumbs
4. Spray with cooking spray and cook in the air fryer for 10 minutes
5. Turnover with tongs and cook for a further 2 minutes

Egg Fried Rice

Servings:2
Cooking Time:15 Minutes

Ingredients:

- 400 g / 14 oz cooked white or brown rice
- 100 g / 3.5 oz fresh peas and sweetcorn
- 2 tbsp olive oil
- 2 eggs, scrambled

Directions:

1. Preheat the air fryer to 150 °C / 300 °F and line the bottom of the basket with parchment paper.
2. In a bowl, mix the cooked white or brown rice and the fresh peas and sweetcorn.
3. Pour in 2 tbsp olive oil and toss to coat evenly. Stir in the scrambled eggs.
4. Transfer the egg rice into the lined air fryer basket, close the lid, and cook for 15 minutes until the eggs are cooked and the rice is soft.
5. Serve as a side dish with some cooked meat or tofu.

Super Easy Fries

Servings: 2
Cooking Time:xx
Ingredients:
- 500g potatoes cut into ½ inch sticks
- 1 tsp olive oil
- ¼ tsp salt
- ¼ tsp pepper

Directions:
1. Place the potatoes in a bowl cover with water and allow to soak for 30 minutes
2. Spread the butter onto one side of the bread slices
3. Pat dry with paper, drizzle with oil and toss to coat
4. Place in the air fryer and cook at 200ºC for about 15 minutes, keep tossing through cooking time
5. Sprinkle with salt and pepper

Zingy Roasted Carrots

Servings: 4
Cooking Time:xx
Ingredients:
- 500g carrots
- 1 tsp olive oil
- 1 tsp cayenne pepper
- Salt and pepper for seasoning

Directions:
1. Peel the carrots and cut them into chunks, around 2" in size
2. Preheat your air fryer to 220ºC
3. Add the carrots to a bowl with the olive oil and cayenne and toss to coat
4. Place in the fryer and cook for 15 minutes, giving them a stir halfway through
5. Season before serving

Crispy Cinnamon French Toast

Servings:2
Cooking Time:5 Minutes

Ingredients:

- 4 slices white bread
- 4 eggs
- 200 ml milk (cow's milk, cashew milk, soy milk, or oat milk)
- 2 tbsp granulated sugar
- 1 tsp brown sugar
- 1 tsp vanilla extract
- ½ tsp ground cinnamon

Directions:

1. Preheat your air fryer to 150 °C / 300 °F and line the bottom of the basket with parchment paper.
2. Cut each of the bread slices into 2 even rectangles and set them aside.
3. In a mixing bowl, whisk together the 4 eggs, milk, granulated sugar, brown sugar, vanilla extract, and ground cinnamon.
4. Soak the bread pieces in the egg mixture until they are fully covered and soaked in the mixture.
5. Place the coated bread slices in the lined air fryer, close the lid, and cook for 4-5 minutes until the bread is crispy and golden.
6. Serve the French toast slices with whatever toppings you desire.

Cheesy Garlic Asparagus

Servings: 4
Cooking Time:xx

Ingredients:

- 1 tsp olive oil
- 500g asparagus
- 1 tsp garlic salt
- 1 tbsp grated parmesan cheese
- Salt and pepper for seasoning

Directions:

1. Preheat the air fryer to 270ºC
2. Clean the asparagus and cut off the bottom 1"
3. Pat dry and place in the air fryer, covering with the oil
4. Sprinkle the parmesan and garlic salt on top, seasoning to your liking
5. Cook for between 7 and 10 minutes
6. Add a little extra parmesan over the top before serving

Desserts Recipes

Apple And Cinnamon Empanadas

Servings: 12
Cooking Time:xx

Ingredients:

- 12 empanada wraps
- 2 diced apples
- 2 tbsp honey
- 1 tsp vanilla extract
- 1 tsp cinnamon
- ⅛ tsp nutmeg
- Olive oil spray
- 2 tsp cornstarch
- 1 tsp water

Directions:

1. Place apples, cinnamon, honey, vanilla and nutmeg in a pan cook for 2-3 minutes until apples are soft
2. Mix the cornstarch and water add to the pan and cook for 30 seconds
3. Add the apple mix to each of the empanada wraps
4. Roll the wrap in half, pinch along the edges, fold the edges in then continue to roll to seal
5. Place in the air fryer and cook at 200ºC for 8 minutes, turn and cook for another 10 minutes

Cinnamon Bites

Servings: 8
Cooking Time:xx

Ingredients:

- 200g flour
- 200g whole wheat flour
- 2 tbsp sugar
- 1 tsp baking powder
- ¼ tsp cinnamon
- 3 tbsp water
- ¼ tsp salt
- 4 tbsp butter
- 25ml milk
- Cooking spray
- 350g powdered sugar

Directions:

1. Mix together flour, sugar, baking powder and salt in a bowl
2. Add the butter and mix well
3. Add the milk and mix to form a dough
4. Knead until dough is smooth, cut into 16 pieces
5. Roll each piece into a small ball
6. Coat the air fryer with cooking spray and heat to 175ºC
7. Add the balls to the air fryer and cook for 12 minutes
8. Mix the powdered sugar and water together, decorate

Butter Cake

Servings: 4
Cooking Time:xx

Ingredients:

- Cooking spray
- 7 tbsp butter
- 25g white sugar
- 2 tbsp white sugar
- 1 egg
- 300g flour
- Pinch salt
- 6 tbsp milk

Directions:

1. Preheat air fryer to 175ºC
2. Spray a small fluted tube pan with cooking spray
3. Beat the butter and all of the sugar together in a bowl until creamy
4. Add the egg and mix until fluffy, add the salt and flour mix well. Add the milk and mix well
5. Put the mix in the pan and cook in the air fryer for 15 minutes

Profiteroles

Servings: 9
Cooking Time:xx

Ingredients:

- 100g butter
- 200g plain flour
- 6 eggs
- 300ml water
- 2 tsp vanilla extract
- 300ml whipped cream
- 100g milk chocolate
- 2 tbsp whipped cream
- 50g butter
- 2 tsp icing sugar

Directions:

1. Preheat the air fryer to 170ºC
2. Place the butter and water in a pan over a medium heat, bring to the boil, remove from the heat and stir in the flour
3. Return to the heat stirring until a dough is formed
4. Mix in the eggs and stir until mixture is smooth, make into profiterole shapes and cook in the air fryer for 10 minutes
5. For the filling whisk together 300ml whipped cream, vanilla extract and the icing sugar
6. For the topping place the butter, 2tbsp whipped cream and chocolate in a bowl and melt over a pan of hot water until mixed together
7. Pipe the filling into the roles and finish off with a chocolate topping

Apple And Cinnamon Puff Pastry Pies

Servings:8
Cooking Time:20 Minutes
Ingredients:

- 4 tbsp butter
- 4 tbsp white sugar
- 2 tbsp brown sugar
- 1 tsp cinnamon
- 1 tsp nutmeg
- 1 tsp salt
- 4 apples, peeled and diced
- 2 large sheets puff pastry
- 1 egg

Directions:

1. Preheat the air fryer to 180 °C / 350 °F. Remove the mesh basket from the machine and line it with parchment paper.
2. In a bowl, whisk together the butter, white sugar, brown sugar, cinnamon, nutmeg, and salt.
3. Place the apples in a heatproof baking dish and coat them in the butter and sugar mixture. Transfer to the air fryer and cook for 10 minutes.
4. Meanwhile, roll out the pastry on a clean, floured surface. Cut the sheets into 8 equal parts.
5. Once the apples are hot and softened, evenly spread the mixture between the pastry sheets. Fold the sheets over to cover the apple and gently press the edges using a fork or your fingers to seal the mixture in.
6. Beat the egg in a bowl and use a brush to coat the top of each pastry sheet.
7. Carefully transfer the filled pastry sheets to the prepared air fryer basket, close the lid, and cook for 10 minutes until the pastry is golden and crispy.

Shortbread Cookies

Servings: 2
Cooking Time:xx
Ingredients:

- 250g flour
- 75g sugar
- 175g butter
- 1 tbsp vanilla essence
- Chocolate buttons for decoration

Directions:

1. Preheat air fryer to 180ºC
2. Place all ingredients apart from the chocolate into a bowl and rub together
3. Form into dough and roll out. Cut into heart shapes using a cookie cutter
4. Place in the air fryer and cook for 10 minutes
5. Place the chocolate buttons onto the shortbread and cook for another 10 minutes at 160ºC

Melting Moments

Servings: 9
Cooking Time:xx

Ingredients:

- 100g butter
- 75g caster sugar
- 150g self raising flour
- 1 egg
- 50g white chocolate
- 3 tbsp desiccated coconut
- 1 tsp vanilla essence

Directions:

1. Preheat the air fryer to 180ºC
2. Cream together the butter and sugar, beat in the egg and vanilla
3. Bash the white chocolate into small pieces
4. Add the flour and chocolate and mix well
5. Roll into 9 small balls and cover in coconut
6. Place in the air fryer and cook for 8 minutes and a further 6 minutes at 160ºC

Oat-covered Banana Fritters

Servings: 4
Cooking Time:xx

Ingredients:

- 3 tablespoons plain/all-purpose flour (gluten-free if you wish)
- 1 egg, beaten
- 90 g/3 oz. oatcakes (gluten-free if you wish) or oat-based cookies, crushed to a crumb consistency
- 1½ teaspoons ground cinnamon
- 1 tablespoon unrefined sugar
- 4 bananas, peeled

Directions:

1. Preheat the air-fryer to 180ºC/350ºF.
2. Set up three bowls – one with flour, one with beaten egg and the other with the oatcake crumb, cinnamon and sugar mixed together. Coat the bananas in flour, then in egg, then in the crumb mixture.
3. Add the bananas to the preheated air-fryer and air-fry for 10 minutes. Serve warm.

Pistachio Brownies

Servings: 4
Cooking Time:xx

Ingredients:

- 75ml milk
- ½ tsp vanilla extract
- 25g salt
- 25g pecans
- 75g flour
- 75g sugar
- 25g cocoa powder
- 1 tbsp ground flax seeds

Directions:

1. Mix all of the dry ingredients together, in another bowl mix the wet ingredients
2. Add all the ingredients together and mix well
3. Preheat the air fryer to 175ºC
4. Line a 5 inch cake tin with parchment paper
5. Pour the brownie mix into the cake tin and cook in the air fryer for about 20 minutes

Milk And White Chocolate Chip Air Fryer Donuts With Frosting

Servings:4
Cooking Time:10 Minutes
Ingredients:

- For the donuts:
- 200 ml milk (any kind)
- 50 g / 3.5 oz brown sugar
- 50 g / 3.5 oz granulated sugar
- 1 tbsp active dry yeast
- 2 tbsp olive oil
- 4 tbsp butter, melted
- 1 egg, beaten
- 1 tsp vanilla extract
- 400 g / 14 oz plain flour
- 4 tbsp cocoa powder
- 100 g / 3.5 oz milk chocolate chips
- For the frosting:
- 5 tbsp powdered sugar
- 2 tbsp cocoa powder
- 100 ml heavy cream
- 50 g / 1.8 oz white chocolate chips, melted

Directions:

1. To make the donuts, whisk together the milk, brown and granulated sugars, and active dry yeast in a bowl. Set aside for a few minutes while the yeast starts to get foamy.
2. Stir the melted butter, beaten egg, and vanilla extract into the bowl. Mix well until all of the ingredients are combined.
3. Fold in the plain flour and cocoa powder until a smooth mixture forms.
4. Lightly flour a clean kitchen top surface and roll the dough out. Gently knead the dough for 2-3 minutes until it becomes soft and slightly tacky.
5. Transfer the dough into a large mixing bowl and cover it with a clean tea towel or some tinfoil. Leave the dough to rise for around one hour in a warm place.
6. Remove the tea towel or tinfoil from the bowl and roll it out on a floured surface once again. Use a rolling pin to roll the dough into a one-inch thick circle.
7. Use a round cookie cutter to create circular donuts and place each one into a lined air fryer basket.
8. Once all of the donuts have been placed into the air fryer, turn the machine onto 150 °C / 300 °F and close the lid.
9. Cook the donuts for 8-10 minutes until they are slightly golden and crispy on the outside.
10. While the donuts are cooking in the air fryer, make the frosting by combining the powdered sugar, cocoa powder, heavy cream, and melted white chocolate chips in a bowl. Mix well until a smooth, sticky mixture forms.
11. When the donuts are cooked, remove them from the air fryer and set aside to cool for 5-10 minutes. Once cooled, evenly spread some frosting on the top layer of each one. Place in the fridge to set for at least one hour.
12. Enjoy the donuts hot or cold.

Peach Pies

Servings: 8
Cooking Time:xx
Ingredients:

- 2 peaches, peeled and chopped
- 1 tbsp lemon juice
- 3 tbsp sugar
- 1 tsp vanilla extract
- ¼ tsp salt
- 1 tsp cornstarch
- 1 pack of shortcrust pastry

Directions:

1. Stir together peaches, lemon juice, sugar, vanilla and salt allow to stand for 15 minutes
2. Drain the peaches keeping 1 tbsp of the juice
3. Mix the liquid with the cornstarch and mix into the peaches
4. Cut out 8 4 inch circles from the pastry. Add 1 tbsp of peach mix to each piece of pastry
5. Fold the dough over to create half moons, crimp the edges with a fork to seal. Spray with cooking spray
6. Place in the air fryer and cook at 180°C for 12-14 minutes

White Chocolate And Raspberry Loaf

Servings:8
Cooking Time:1 Hour 10 Minutes
Ingredients:

- 400 g / 14 oz plain flour
- 2 tsp baking powder
- 1 tsp ground cinnamon
- ½ tsp salt
- 3 eggs, beaten
- 50 g / 3.5 oz granulated sugar
- 50 g / 3.5 oz brown sugar
- 100 g / 3.5 oz white chocolate chips
- 100 g / 3.5 oz fresh raspberries
- 1 tbsp cocoa powder
- 4 tbsp milk
- 1 tsp vanilla extract

Directions:

1. Preheat the air fryer to 150 °C / 300 °F and line a loaf tin with parchment paper.
2. Combine the plain flour, baking powder, ground cinnamon, and salt in a large mixing bowl.
3. Whisk eggs into the bowl, then stir in the granulated sugar and brown sugar. Mix well before folding in the white chocolate chips, fresh raspberries, cocoa powder, milk, and vanilla extract.
4. Stir the mixture until it is lump-free and transfer into a lined loaf tin. Place the loaf tin into the lined air fryer basket, close the lid, and cook for 30-40 minutes.
5. The cake should be golden and set by the end of the cooking process. Insert a knife into the centre of the cake. It should come out dry when the cake is fully cooked.
6. Remove the cake from the air fryer, still in the loaf tin. Set aside to cool on a drying rack for 20-30 minutes before cutting into slices and serving.

Banana Cake

Servings: 4
Cooking Time:xx
Ingredients:

- Cooking spray
- 25g brown sugar
- ½ tbsp butter
- 1 banana, mashed
- 1 egg
- 2 tbsp honey
- 225g self raising flour
- ½ tsp cinnamon
- Pinch salt

Directions:

1. Preheat air fryer to 160°C
2. Spray a small fluted tube tray with cooking spray
3. Beat sugar and butter together in a bowl until creamy
4. Combine the banana egg and honey together in another bowl
5. Mix into the butter until smooth
6. Sift in the remaining ingredients and mix well
7. Spoon into the tray and cook in the air fryer for 30 minutes

New York Cheesecake

Servings: 8
Cooking Time:xx

Ingredients:

- 225g plain flour
- 100g brown sugar
- 100g butter
- 50g melted butter
- 1 tbsp vanilla essence
- 750g soft cheese
- 2 cups caster sugar
- 3 large eggs
- 50ml quark

Directions:

1. Add the flour, sugar, and 100g butter to a bowl and mix until combined. Form into biscuit shapes place in the air fryer and cook for 15 minutes at 180ºC
2. Grease a springform tin
3. Break the biscuits up and mix with the melted butter, press firmly into the tin
4. Mix the soft cheese and sugar in a bowl until creamy, add the eggs and vanilla and mix. Mix in the quark
5. Pour the cheesecake batter into the pan
6. Place in your air fryer and cook for 30 minutes at 180ºC. Leave in the air fryer for 30 minutes whilst it cools
7. Refrigerate for 6 hours

Cinnamon Biscuit Bites

Servings: 16
Cooking Time:xx

Ingredients:

- 200g flour
- 200g wholewheat flour
- 2 tbsp sugar
- 1 tsp baking powder
- ¼ tsp cinnamon
- ¼ tsp salt
- 4 tbsp butter
- 50ml milk
- Cooking spray
- 300g icing sugar
- 3 tbsp water

Directions:

1. Mix together flour, salt, sugar baking powder and cinnamon in a bowl
2. Add butter and mix until well combined
3. Add milk and form a dough, place dough on a floured surface and knead until smooth
4. Cut into 16 equal pieces and form each piece into a ball
5. Place in the air fryer and cook at 180ºC for about 12 minutes
6. Mix together icing sugar and water and coat to serve

Apple Chips With Yogurt Dip

Servings: 4
Cooking Time:xx

Ingredients:

- 1 apple
- 1 tsp cinnamon
- 2 tsp oil
- Cooking spray
- 25g greek yogurt
- 1 tbsp almond butter
- 1 tsp honey

Directions:

1. Thinly slice the apple, place in a bowl and coat with cinnamon and oil
2. Coat the air fryer with cooking spray and add the apple slices
3. Cook the slices for 12 minutes at 180ºC
4. Mix the butter, honey and yogurt together and serve with the apple slices as a dip

Cinnamon-maple Pineapple Kebabs

Servings: 2
Cooking Time:xx

Ingredients:

- 4 x pineapple strips, roughly 2 x 2 cm/¾ x ¾ in. by length of pineapple
- 1 teaspoon maple syrup
- ½ teaspoon vanilla extract
- ¼ teaspoon ground cinnamon
- Greek or plant-based yogurt and grated lime zest, to serve

Directions:

1. Line the air-fryer with an air-fryer liner or a piece of pierced parchment paper. Preheat the air-fryer to 180ºC/350ºF.
2. Stick small metal skewers through the pineapple lengthways. Mix the maple syrup and vanilla extract together, then drizzle over the pineapple and sprinkle over the cinnamon.
3. Add the skewers to the preheated lined air-fryer and air-fry for 15 minutes, turning once. If there is any maple-vanilla mixture left after the initial drizzle, then drizzle this over the pineapple during cooking too. Serve with yogurt and lime zest.

Banana Bread

Servings: 8
Cooking Time:xx

Ingredients:

- 200g flour
- 1 tsp cinnamon
- ½ tsp salt
- ¼ tsp baking soda
- 2 ripe banana mashed
- 2 large eggs
- 75g sugar
- 25g plain yogurt
- 2 tbsp oil
- 1 tsp vanilla extract
- 2 tbsp chopped walnuts
- Cooking spray

Directions:

1. Line a 6 inch cake tin with parchment paper and coat with cooking spray
2. Whisk together flour, cinnamon, salt and baking soda set aside
3. In another bowl mix together remaining ingredients, add the flour mix and combine well
4. Pour batter into the cake tin and place in the air fryer
5. Cook at 155ºC for 35 minutes turning halfway through

Peanut Butter And Banana Bites

Servings: 12
Cooking Time:xx
Ingredients:

- 1 banana
- 12 wonton wrappers
- 75g peanut butter
- 1-2 tsp vegetable oil

Directions:

1. Slice the banana and place in a bowl of water with lemon juice to prevent browning
2. Place one piece of banana and a spoon of peanut butter in each wonton wrapper
3. Wet the edges of each wrapper and fold over to seal
4. Spray the air fryer with oil
5. Place in the air fryer and cook at 190ºC for 6 minutes

Apple Fritters

Servings: 4
Cooking Time:xx
Ingredients:

- 225g self raising flour
- 200g greek yogurt
- 2 tsp sugar
- 1 tbsp cinnamon
- 1 apple peeled and chopped
- 225g icing sugar
- 2 tbsp milk

Directions:

1. Mix the flour, yogurt, sugar, cinnamon and apple together. Knead for about 3 -4 minutes
2. Mix the icing sugar and milk together to make the glaze and set aside
3. Line the air fryer with parchment paper and spray with cooking spray
4. Divide the fritter mix into four, flatten each portion and place in the air fryer
5. Cook at 185ºC for about 15 minutes turning halfway
6. Drizzle with glaze to serve

Cherry Pies

Servings: 6
Cooking Time:xx
Ingredients:

- 300g prepared shortcrust pastry
- 75g cherry pie filling
- Cooking spray
- 3 tbsp icing sugar
- ½ tsp milk

Directions:

1. Cut out 6 pies with a cookie cutter
2. Add 1 ½ tbsp filling to each pie
3. Fold the dough in half and seal around the edges with a fork
4. Place in the air fryer, spray with cooking spray
5. Cook at 175ºC for 10 minutes
6. Mix icing sugar and milk and drizzled over cooled pies to serve

S'mores

Servings: 2
Cooking Time:xx
Ingredients:

- 2 graham crackers, broken in half
- 2 marshmallows, halved
- 2 pieces of chocolate

Directions:

1. Place 2 halves of graham crackers in the air fryer and add a marshmallow to each sticky side down
2. Cook in the air fryer at 180ºC for 5 minutes until the marshmallows are golden
3. Remove from the air fryer add a piece of chocolate and top with the other half of graham crackers

Appendix : Recipes Index

G

H

J

K

L

M

N

O

P

Q

R

S

T

V

W

Z

Printed in Great Britain
by Amazon

27216619R00051